WOMEN WHO HEAR VOICES

WOMEN WHO HEAR VOICES

The Challenge of Religious Experience

SIDNEY CALLAHAN

**2003 Madeleva Lecture
in Spirituality**

PAULIST PRESS
New York/Mahwah, New Jersey

ISBN: 0-8091-4198-1

Published by Paulist Press
997 Macarthur Boulevard
Mahwah, New Jersey 07430

www.paulistpress.com

Printed and bound in the
United States of America

HEAR VOICES **WOMEN WHO HEAR VOICES** Women Who Hear Voices WOMEN WHO HEAR VOICES **WOMEN WHO HEAR VOICES** Women Who Hear Voices WOMEN WHO HEAR VOICES **WOMEN WHO HEAR VOICES** Women Who Hear Voices WOMEN WHO HEAR VOICES **WOMEN WHO HEAR VOICES** Women Who Hear Voices WOMEN WHO HEAR VOICES **WOMEN WHO HEAR VOICES** Women Who Hear Voices WOMEN WHO HEAR VOICES **WOMEN WHO HEAR VOICES** Women Who Hear Voices WOMEN WHO HEAR VOICES **WOMEN WHO HEAR VOICES** Women Who Hear Voices WOMEN WHO HEAR VOICES **WOMEN WHO HEAR VOICES** Women Who Hear Voices WOMEN WHO HEAR VOICES **WOMEN WHO HEAR VOICES** Women Who Hear Voices WOMEN WHO HEAR VOICES **WOMEN WHO HEAR VOICES** Women Who Hear Voices WOMEN WHO HEAR VOICES **WOMEN WHO HEAR VOICES** Women Who Hear Voices WOMEN WHO HEAR VOICES **WOMEN WHO HEAR VOICES** Women Who Hear Voices WOMEN WHO HEAR VOICES **WOMEN WHO HEAR VOICES** Women Who Hear Voices WOMEN WHO HEAR VOICES **WOMEN WHO HEAR VOICES** Women Who Hear Voices WOMEN WHO HEAR VOICES **WOMEN WHO HEAR VOICES** Women Who Hear

Sidney Callahan, Ph.D., is an author, professor and licensed psychologist. She earned her B.A. in English (magna cum laude) from Bryn Mawr College, her M.A. in psychology from Sarah Lawrence College and her Ph.D. in social and personality psychology from the City College of New York. Callahan has written many articles, books and columns devoted to religious, psychological and ethical questions. She has been awarded many honors in the course of her career and served on many boards. For twenty years she taught and served as a tenured professor of psychology; she has also held visiting chairs of interdisciplinary studies and moral theology at Georgetown in Washington, D.C., and St. John's University in New York City. Sidney and Daniel Callahan have been married since 1954 and have six grown children and four grandchildren.

WOMEN WHO HEAR VOICES

*Introduction: Basic Questions
and Personal Interest*

> When his family heard it, they went out to
> restrain him, for people were saying, "He
> has gone out of his mind." (Mark 3:21)

Suspicions that religious beliefs and fervent religious experiences are a form of mental pathology
still prevail in our world. Disciples can expect to
receive no better treatment than their master, but
Christian women in particular have been more generally accused of being neurotic and subject to illusions and delusions. But why should we be
surprised that women's experiences have been discounted? The tendency to denigrate women has
marked the history of Western civilization.
Misogyny marred ancient civilizations, and during
the centuries in which the Catholic Church developed, misogyny grew to thoroughly infect Christian
thought and practice. For these sins of the church
against women the present pope has apologized.

For centuries Catholic theologians assumed that Eve and her daughters were guilty of the sin that initiated the fall of humankind. Patriarchal readings of the scriptures were common practice, and all the negative references to women in the Old Testament were emphasized. Although Eve and Adam both sinned in the garden and many heroic women are depicted in scripture, those passages declaring men and women to be equal in God's sight were slighted. Women were blamed as a dangerous gateway to evil and assumed to be naturally inferior to men in both intellect and morals. In the New Testament remains of antifeminism can be found. Under the influence of ancient Greek views of human nature, a dualism of body and mind was affirmed. A spiritual eternal soul was thought to be imprisoned in a vulnerable dying body. The soul would only be liberated at death from being chained to a corpse. When the body is thought to be fundamentally impure and a constant hindrance to the soul's ascent, women, with their reproductive bodies, will be disparaged. Feminine physical functions will necessarily produce uncleanness and impurity. Women will end up categorized as more like animals than males. As inferior, unclean and morally suspect, it follows that women, along with children, should be governed by males in the family, the state and the church.

But all of this sad history of women's mistreatment does not have to be rehearsed at length here.

At this point feminist scholarship has analyzed the countless ways that male-dominated groups have kept women subordinated. Crude exercises of physical power have been accompanied by subtle psychological processes that have served to justify women's suppression. Women have been categorized as the Other, the second sex, and readily become the objects of projection, fantasy and stereotyping. Males wielding power have had to justify their position by maintaining a belief in their superiority. In fact, any dominated group must be characterized by their oppressors as deserving their fate and deprivations. Those excluded from power will be seen as possessing those weak and inferior human characteristics that cannot be acknowledged by the ruling male elite.[1] Women, like blacks, Jews, Indians, gypsies or other outcasts, will be designated to embody the problematic unacknowledged vulnerabilities of humankind. The excluded will be seen as emotional, erotic, sexually unrestrained, neurotic, unintellectual, fickle, vain, timid, childlike, superstitious and generally less morally developed. They will be thought to be closer to the earth, more nurturing, more religious and more given to singing and dancing. They have rhythm, if not a highly developed rationality. Their weak suggestible natures will naturally be more likely to have questionable religious experiences. While inferiors can serve and work well when properly led and supervised, it would be folly to share power or governance with them.

Out-groups who have been denied equality must stay firmly identified as inferior by the eternal dictates of nature. As Aristotle famously declared, some men (and most women?) are born to be slaves.

Other subtle strategies of exclusion in regard to women have been invented due to their sexual and reproductive powers. After all, women's mysterious procreative potentialities are needed to reproduce the dominant male elite and to share their domestic and sexual lives. Consequently, women often have been invested with value and significance in their family roles. The nurturing of a mother necessary in the beginning of each life can produce a residue of influence springing from positive bonds of affection. In Western civilization women have been the subject of positive gender stereotypes that have given birth to "romantic feminism," which emphasizes the positive differences between men and women. In this "difference feminism" approach, women are thought to be morally and emotionally superior to males. But they can still end up being denied full public equality because they are too nurturing, too fine, too sensitive or spiritual to be capable of, or sullied by, the tough demands of public leadership or governance. Let women remain protected at home, raising children, acting as helpmates to their husbands and providing for the community's cultural and religious needs of the heart. Women can be the house angels. At home, in church and in their private lives women can freely flourish as they exercise their womanly gifts. They need not be subject to the public pressures that result in distorting their essentially feminine nature.

This confinement to a pedestal has been founded on positive stereotypes but can be just as stunting of individual gifts and talents as overt bias and discrimination. Those women who have rebelled against the constraining stereotypes assigned to them in either secular or religious life have found themselves punished and labeled as unnatural women who are neurotically unbalanced. Unfortunately, positive stereotypes often grow out of a basic ambivalence and can quickly flip from an idealized overvaluation to the negative opposite of hostile bias. With women, ambivalence shows itself in the familiar saint-or-whore, Eve-or-Mary polarity. As one modern feminist biblical scholar puts it while analyzing the fluctuating reputation in church history of Mary Magdalene, strong women in public roles have often been identified as "a whore, a prostitute, and yes a madwoman as all of us women are or are in danger of being labeled...."[2]

Mary Magdalene's case is an instructive one in showing the problems surrounding women's religious experience. Originally, in the gospels Mary Magdalene is cured by Jesus of her seven demons (psychosis or seven sins?) and becomes his faithful follower, using her financial means to provide support for her rabboni and the disciples. Mary and other women traveled with Jesus and at the end stood steadfastly at the foot of the cross. Mary was the first to learn the miraculous good news of the resurrection and was sent to give the message to the rest of the apostles. She was the "apostle to the apostles," although the testimony of women was culturally and legally disallowed at the time. Not surprisingly, some of the disciples doubted the women's account of this news that was too good to be true. Feminist biblical scholars also provide evidence that Mary appears to have acted as a leader of an early community of Christian disciples.[3] However, in the following centuries Mary's image among Western Christians became falsely identified with that of another woman in another story, that of the penitent prostitute who washes Jesus' feet with her tears and dries them with her hair. The image of the Magdalene as a reformed prostitute or courtesan retained a tainted feminine aura of dangerous eroticism and neurotic extremism. Like Lord Byron, Mary had been seen as "mad, bad and dangerous to know." After her conversion the Magdalene was depicted in Western Catholic folklore as a romantic and dramatic figure. In today's popular secular folklore, as in the musical of *Jesus Christ Superstar,* it is easier to think of Mary Magdalene as a sexual paramour of Jesus than as his strong, faithful coworker who becomes a leader of the early church. The history of Mary Magdalene's reputation is symbolic of the tendency to subsume women's religious experience in feminine stereotypes of erotic neurosis.

If such disciples as Mary Magdalene have been accused of near madness with an erotic cast, it should be no surprise that similarly reductionist dismissive views have been applied to other intensely religious women. Joan of Arc, for one, was fatally rejected and burned because of her fidelity to her religious experience of voices giving her guidance from God. Joan in her own time was also accused by her defeated English enemies as being a harlot and a witch. Finally, she could be officially discounted after being designated a heretic and an unnatural woman who returned to heresy and the wearing of male clothes in prison. (This last "offense" was her defense against prison rape and not a statement relating to her gender, since Joan fervently believed that God had chosen her as the maid to free France.) Happily, Joan the executed heretic was rather quickly rehabilitated, but largely with the help of French political influence. Later she was named a saint by the church that had condemned her and turned her over to the secular arm to be burned at the stake. Unfortunately, many other women who refused to repudiate their private religious experiences were never rehabilitated or vindicated after their brutal executions as heretics or witches.

But even Joan the heroic maid, despite her extraordinary meteoric achievements and down-to-earth common sense, has been diagnosed as neurotic or psychotic by secular thinkers. At the end of the nineteenth century the famous French novelist Zola could dub Joan "a 'hysterical peasant girl' whose dreamy-eyed interpreters were ignoring the 'scientific truth.'"[4] The scientific truth then and now was clear to certain secular observers: Joan and other religious women were suffering erotically tinged neuroses and self-delusions in their intense religious experiences. The secular mind is challenged by trying to diagnose the degree and type of pathology in question. Also of interest is the exploration of which social and cultural superstitions can give authority to women's hysterical manifestations. Of course in the eyes of unbelievers those males who report mystical experience also should be dismissed as deluded, but the common judgment was that one finds "affective and erotic forms of mysticism associated with women and more speculative or intellectual forms of mysticism associated with men."[5] "Affective and erotic" elements are the problematic characteristics seen to infect women's religious experience. In certain ideologies defining human nature, feminine emotions and embodiment have been suspect as inferior and dangerous to the rational organization of personality and society. While church and state no longer collude to burn heretics or hang witches, women's

religious experiences can still be readily discounted. Not a lot has changed from that confident
secular period when another nineteenth-century
observer of St. Teresa of Avila could sarcastically
note, "it is significant that the miraculous manifestations of the Romish Church should have been
vouchsafed only to women whose constitu-
tion...was thoroughly broken down by years of
agonizing disease."[6] Even so sympathetic an
observer of religion and saintliness as William
James could complain of St. Teresa of Avila that
"in the main her idea of religion seems to have
been that of an endless amatory flirtation...
between the devotee and the deity."[7] James, while
a stalwart defender of religious experience, was
also an advocate of manliness, individualism, religious seriousness and the strenuous life. He found
many Roman Catholic female saints to be effemi-
nate, unintellectual, neurotic, narrow and espous-
ing "paltry" narratives in their childish worship
filled with toylike ritual objects. James was no fan
of sacramental liturgies.

Today, in a therapeutic psychological and neurological age, secular opponents of religion have
more elaborate kinds of reductive explanations
for women's religious experience. A typical example can be found in the assertion of psychiatrist-
writer Oliver Sacks that Hildegard of Bingen's
visions were due to migraine headaches, with
their typical "dramatic disturbances in vision and

the visual field, taking the form of strange and often twinkling brilliances."[8] Sacks is a sympathetic agnostic humanist who always attempts to show how his patients make efforts to transcend their brain pathologies. Thus he does credit Hildegard with a high degree of creativity in her response to her neurological disorder. And he cautions that, with visions, "It is impossible to ascertain in the vast majority of cases, whether the experience represents a hysterical or psychotic ecstasy, the effects of intoxication or an epileptic or migrainous manifestation."[9]

This list of options includes most of the medical pathological conditions in which hallucinations appear, with the omission of intense stress, prolonged perceptual deprivation, hypnosis or other induced states of altered consciousness. Significantly, having an authentic revelation from God does not make the list of explanations. The best a visionary saint can do is to creatively mitigate her brain disease. The possibility of having nonpathological hallucinations or visions is not mentioned. In Hildegard's case, despite the passage of centuries, Sacks is quite confident of the diagnosis of migraine disease. He offers as evidence some of the patterns in Hildegard's depictions of her visions, selectively culled from the hundreds of pages of her voluminous accounts. For Sacks, the ecstatic and rapturously intense reactions as well as the auras surrounding such episodes of hallucinatory visions are engendered by her underlying pathology. For good measure, Sacks throws in the "historical parallel" of Fyodor Dosteovsky's reactions during his "ecstatic epileptic auras." Temporal-lobe epilepsy presents another popular explanation of the pathological source of rapturous religious experiences.

While Sacks may appear to be rather simplistic in his "retrospective diagnosis" across cultural and religious ideologies, he is following widespread current psychiatric approaches that categorize the hearing of voices and the seeing of visions as symptoms of some psychotic disorder, brain damage or toxic poisoning. Popular accounts of LSD, peyote or other drug "trips" have made modern populations familiar with temporary episodes of drug-induced hallucinations. Ecstatic "highs" or ecstasies are commonly experienced by users of euphoria-inducing drugs and by patients suffering from psychotic episodes of mania or less severe hypomanic reactions. Moreover, widespread claims resulting from the New-Age practice of channeling voices from the "other world" of spirits have made middle-class Americans familiar with trances and with the potential effects of meditation in creating altered states of consciousness. With globalization we now recognize that trances are more common in many other cultures. Shamans and other spiritual healers have induced trances and been studied by both anthropologists and by students of the brain and consciousness.[10]

In the twentieth century, scientific investigations using new brain imaging techniques have begun to explore altered states of consciousness, starting with sleep and dreaming and going on to studies of meditating adepts. One result of this is the slowly emerging understanding that altered states of consciousness and trances, whether induced or spontaneous, need not always be diagnosed as psychotic. But under the reigning rationalism of Western eyes, altered states are definitely seen as dangerous and undesirable. Are not those who are asleep and dreaming acknowledged to be severely impaired when it comes to reality testing or adaptive functioning? If human persons were asleep all the time or subject to frequent ecstatic trances, they would be unlikely to survive. Yes, a certain amount of sleep is necessary for human survival, but as yet, no one fully understands why this odd withdrawal from reality has evolved in the brain/mind.

So too, the functions of dreaming are hotly disputed—is the brain clearing out its garbage, or consolidating memories, or creating scenarios to match the cycling of emotions? (Jungian and Freudian theories of dreams and the mind, along with most of their other theories, are now passé in most academic circles.) Dreams are the most basic and universal form of an altered state of consciousness but, as in psychotic episodes, the dreamer lacks the waking ability of reality testing. While the dreaming individual in a trance-like state can construct scenarios, he loses contact with everyday consensual reality. As one psychiatric sleep researcher has put it, every one of us goes crazy every night.[11] Mental illness has been seen as a brain disorder that can be characterized by involuntary uncontrolled dreaming in a seemingly wakeful state. The impaired individual loses the ability to truly wake up. History may or may not be a nightmare from which we cannot awake, but psychosis is probably more so. Horror-filled psychotic states can be like the worst of nightmares. Pleasant dreams are also delusions but do not create the same kind of emotional suffering. But while neither psychotic euphoria nor drug-induced euphoria creates short-term suffering, both are ultimately dangerous because they impair reality testing and provide an escape from necessary tasks. Addictions, with their euphoric illusions, destroy lives, and hostile critics do not hesitate to label religious practices as a form of addiction. At this point the harmful pathology of addiction is clearly apparent, although no one yet fully understands how addictions originate. The causes of addiction, psychosis, dreams or other altered states of consciousness are conceded to be puzzles involving the interactions of genes, behaviors and social conditioning.

Yet enough is known of the pathology of altered states of consciousness to engender suspicion of religious experiences, especially intense religious experiences. The ecstasies reported by worshipers or those in prayer can easily be identified with the manic episodes of psychosis. Religious practices and rituals can be seen as a form of self-reinforcing addiction that encourages escapism. Reports of hearing God's voice or God's messages, whether ecstatic or punishing, can easily be judged as resulting from a pathological dream-like hallucinatory state. In fact many stories of human encounters with the Divine (as with Abraham, Samuel, Peter, John, various other saints, etc.) involve dreams or voluntarily induced altered states of consciousness brought on by fasting, isolation or meditation. When the brain is known to be capable of creating visions under various conditions, why bring God into the process of explanation? Similarly, claims for the existence of demons and demonic possession are dismissed. Once it is known that an impaired or intoxicated or highly suggestible mind can create horrible hallucinations of persecuting voices or induce involuntary tics or spasms or create alternate identities in dissociated states, it is no longer necessary to see Satan or demons as the cause. Dissociated identity disorders, or what used to be called multiple personality disorders, can produce weird conditions in which different persona with

14

different voices and behaviors are manifested within one individual. The individual may or may not suffer amnesia regarding the coming into consciousness of the other parts of his or her personality. Moviegoers have seen *Sybil* or the *Three Faces of Eve* and know about multiple personality disorders. These strange disorders may or may not originate from the suggestions of eager therapists, but they certainly do resemble descriptions of demonic possession. Films display the popularly understood symptoms of demonic possession. But many psychologists analyze the process of "possession" as an actual loss of control or self-monitoring of one part of the mind over the other.[12] At any rate, the existence of strange and disturbing pathological episodes in which an impaired mind loses control of itself and loses contact with its own memories and everyday reality can offer scientific explanations of why people have believed in demons. A belief in demons could help observers understand the strange behaviors that an impaired brain can produce.

But if psychiatrists (and psychologists like me) find it only reasonable to explain away demonic possession as pathological, what is to keep the reductive approach from moving on to explanations of positive spiritual experiences as hallucinatory and illusory self-creations? Knowledge of mental pathology ensures that visions and voices from God and spiritual experiences will inevitably be greeted with grave suspicion. As the old joke has it, it is all right to speak to God, but if God speaks to you, watch out. After all, mental hospitals are filled with persons suffering from delusions and hallucinations concerning the voice of God, the Devil, demons and other supernatural entities. Granted, in many educated theological circles the Devil as a personified personal agent of evil has departed the scene. Today attributions of demonic possession or witchcraft are rare, but diagnoses of mental pathology, suggestibility and altered states of consciousness, with or without amnesias, are increasingly common as explanations of religious experience.

Various reductionist explanations of women's intense religious experiences take other forms that are more psychosocial and less neurological. Many psychoanalytic thinkers following Freud's lead see religious experience of all kinds as arising from the unconscious mind's wish fulfillment and regression to infantile experiences.[13] The infant is hypothesized as having an undifferentiated sense of self that produces a sense of unity with the benevolent nurturing mother. This union is like an "oceanic feeling" of oneness with the universe reported by mystics. A religious person reporting mystical experiences of God or the Infinite is falsely identifying his or her regression into an infantile state. Experiences of a divine presence, along with beliefs in God, are actually products of

16

regression; they represent a flight from rational reality into unconsciously dominated forms of primitive thinking. Persons will take comfort in the illusion that a benevolent deity, like a powerful parent, will fulfill their wishes to be taken care of as well as their need to be forgiven for their sins. Guilt feelings stemming from archaic and intentional lapses into wrongdoing can be assuaged through religious rituals and belief. Finally, and most importantly, skeptics aver that superstitious religious beliefs in immortality help humankind deny the all but unbearable reality that they are going to die. Persons cannot come to terms with the inevitable extinction of self-consciousness, and so religious beliefs are constructed in order to deny and defend against death and the powerless vulnerability of humanity in the face of a remorseless meaningless universe.

Faith protects human consciousness and the human mind from the sad reality that the world has no meaning or purpose. For Freudian atheists, human beings regress to magical thinking and use their mental capacities to construct religious myths that give meaning to life. Only those courageous individuals who take science seriously will be able to commit themselves to the unblinking rational truths of atheism. And for Freudians, more men than women will be among those capable of looking at and accepting the bleakness of the universe. Freud saw women as generally less autonomous and rational because of their course of psychic development. As the result of the sexual dynamics of normal female development, most women will end up less identified with their fathers and less committed to the intellectual, moral and principled standards that mark the highest civilization.

Women would be more given to the emotionally regressed wish fulfillment that characterizes religious belief and experience. As one prominent female Freudian theorist put it in the 1940s (the high tide of Freudian orthodoxy), the feminine core of personality consists of "a harmonious blend of masochism, narcissism and passivity."[14] Narcissism would allow women to imagine that God loves them, and masochism would allow them to take pleasure in the sacrifices demanded by motherhood and religious submission. Passivity facilitates obedience, and so women would naturally be led by men, especially priests. Women would also be more given to wish fulfillment than action. Such psychoanalytic views of women's nature helped to justify the naturalness and the appropriateness of assigning women secondary roles in the family, society and religious communities. Moreover, women's purported eroticism could be seen as the unconscious sexual origin of the ecstasies of female saints. The erotic language used by mystics and the erotic quality of religious ecstasies were seen by psychoanalytic skeptics as obvious substitutes for sexual fulfillment. In other words, much of the psychoanalytic reductionist critique of religion follows "Freud's trajectory of reducing religious concepts to intrapsychic dynamics."[15] Religious experiences and beliefs can be dismissed as defensive phenomena emerging from primitive thinking and wish-fulfilling emotions.

Another more cognitively oriented reductionist theory of religion emphasizes the process by which cognitive constructs are projected upon reality in order to impose meaning upon chaos. Critics with new awareness of the brain's powers of constructing order out of incoming stimuli can view religious beliefs as cognitive constructions of the mind devised to solve puzzling questions arising in the environment. The human brain has been adapted through eons of evolution to solve problems, detect cause and effect and help humans function in their world. Today, the human species possesses an incredible array of different intellectual capacities that develop in programmed ways. In an average expected environment the human infant is ready to learn and develop certain capacities, while being constrained in others. Many different kinds or modules of intelligence are manifested in homo sapiens, the seven major ones, by the count of some theorists, being: linguistic, mathematical, spatial, musical, kinesthetic and intra- and interpersonal intelligences.[16] An innate capacity to feel, read, respond to and control emotions has recently been

19

added to the list as "emotional intelligence."[17] These various human capacities are made possible by the selective evolutionary processes that produce the human species' genetic make-up, and as such will appear always and everywhere in every human group. Some social groups will encourage the development of one or another intelligence, but they all appear everywhere in some degree. Some individuals will have inherited more innate potentiality for some mode of intelligence. Many societies will recognize and develop the innate gifts of their musicians or artists or athletes or sages or strategists. Religions will be constructed as a by-product of the exercise of the different kinds of prescientific intelligences.

Moreover, say skeptics, the environmental niche of the human species is social and interpersonal, so every human group must encourage emotional intelligence or those characteristic emotional behaviors and responses that facilitate group life. Docility and conformity, along with affective bonding have been seen as necessary for cooperative communal life. Religion can be seen as emerging in human life because it satisfies the needs of individuals and groups to exercise intelligence and ensure docility. The mind will inevitably operate to produce explanations and causes for problems and puzzles. Using logical cause-and-effect reasoning, every human group will construct myths and explanatory narratives to understand and cope with the world of natural events and human beings. Therefore, say unbelievers, the fact that religion appears in every human group does not prove anything other than the fact that humans always and everywhere try to cope with a confusing world and ensure group conformity. Moreover, evolutionary processes are driven by self-interest and the push for dominance. Stephen Pinker, one prominent evolutionary psychologist who is hostile to religion, considers that religion arises as a "desperate" and "useless" measure when other rational ways to cope with life have failed. People take constructs from the brain's innate cognitive modules and project them on unexplained realities. But compared to modern science, "religious beliefs are notable for their lack of imagination."[18] In fact, religion is "harmful" and a "waste of time," since it allows persons to be dominated and exploited. Religious beliefs serve the interests of the powerful because "the demand for miracles creates a market that would-be priests compete in, and they can succeed by exploiting people's dependence on experts." Pinker's animus is extreme even in secular academic circles, but he does voice the scorn for religion permitted in modern cultures of unbelief. His complaints are all the more ironic because it is followed by a long discussion admitting that science cannot explain consciousness, the self, free will, meaning, knowledge, morality and music— and may never be able to. He does not see that

these are elements of reality that have had something to do with the persistence of religious belief.
It is easier for him to concur with Mencken that
"Theology is the effort to explain the unknowable
in terms of the not worth knowing."[19]

Pinker's explanation of the universal appear-
ance of religion builds on other received ideas that
religious stories are created to anthropomorphize
the world. Before the advent of science, the human
cognitive ability to solve cause-and-effect problems would naturally result in myths of a creator
or creator gods. Human emotional intelligence
and interpersonal responses of love and anger are
projected upon divinities who will also be thought
to have emotions and engage in purposeful projects. Humans create their gods in their own image,
so naturally familiar emotional responses, attach-
ments and wishes will be projected upon the
Divinity. After all, say skeptics, humans are
known to be adept at creating imaginary agents in
narrative scenarios and dramas. Many children
display this skill in creating imaginary compan-
ions with whom they converse. As one psychological debunker puts it, after an analysis of Edgar
Bergen and his famous puppet-dummy compan-
ion, Charlie McCarthy, "The proclivity to believe
that there is a God, or more than one god, is consistent with our willy-nilly perception of agents
everywhere, although in this case the agent is writ

22

large as an ideal agent, a best possible mind. God may be the ultimate imaginary friend."[20]

Since individual humans can be placated and persuaded, so must the gods be assuaged through gifts and persuasive rituals. In addition, religious worship of the gods is appealing, because believers can make use of the entire range of human abilities for language, music, ritual action and artistic and creative capacities. Music can be seen as particularly effective in arousing ecstatic religious emotional experience since music seems to directly produce emotions in the brain. Music and dance may also have been used by early human groups to produce solidarity and reduce conflicts and tensions. Therefore, religious beliefs and religious rituals have become universal, not because they are true, but because they give the illusion of meaning and satisfy human desires for comfort, conformity and comprehension of the puzzling events of the natural world. Humans are self-interpreting animals, and religion is a universal strategy of interpretation. The accusations made by unbelievers are not only that religions give false consolation by indulging in primitive wish fulfillment, but that religions also claim to provide meaningful answers where none really exist. Once constructed, religious scenarios and stories will be emotionally invested in by groups. Today much published psychological research is devoted to "believed-in imaginings" and the subtle ways that the

23

brain/mind can construct and persevere in false beliefs.[21] Emotions are thought to be given decisive weight in the process of maintaining beliefs and disarming rational evidence.

Individuals persevere in habitual patterns of irrationality through the power of group influence. Social groups give communal support for preserving beliefs that alien abductions and satanic ritual abuse regularly take place in America. New research on false memories can explain how sincere suggestible individuals can have their self-constructed false memories confirmed by a community of believers.[22] Believers will band together against outside skeptics. In secular sociological reductionist approaches to religion, belief in either alien abduction or orthodox Christianity can be readily explained away as serving the function of social cohesion. Whether cult or church, continued existence is assured if each new generation is socialized into group beliefs and practices. Women in their roles as family caretakers will play a large role in preserving a group's belief system. Once a set of common beliefs and expectations are adopted, a powerful force for consistent interpretations for new experience becomes active. Persons will be programmed to attribute certain feelings and thoughts as coming from God or as being inspirations from the Spirit.[23] Unfortunately, the argument of secular social constructionist approaches to religious experience casts doubt upon the belief that a Creator God could directly communicate with human beings. God can be denied to be an effective agent who actually causes religious experiences. No, the erroneous attributions and internalized social judgments of a group are being projected upon internal and external phenomena, so that internal experiences are thought of as coming from God.[24] Human beings construct their religious experiences from the general intellectual beliefs about the universe they have been taught.

In a sociological reductive analysis of religion, women's religious experiences are as handily disparaged as in the neurological or psychoanalytical skeptical path. Since women exercise less social power in a male-dominated system, they will be more open to religious experiences as a compensation for their oppression and as a potential route to influence and gain social attention. Compensation and consolation can come from the belief that in the next world the sufferings of women and others oppressed here below will be made good. On the way to heaven it can also be the case that religion can offer women access to social power in this world. If women can claim communications from God in the Spirit, they can lay claim to authority denied them in other domains. Have not women often used religion and religious groups to justify their exercise of agency and initiative beyond their constrained roles? No one would have listened to

Joan of Arc without her claim to supernatural voices. Many other female saints and mystics have relied on the authority of religious experience to embark upon enlarged spheres of activity in male-dominated circles—creating and organizing institutions, raising money, dealing with secular and religious authorities, writing, teaching, counseling and traveling around on pilgrimages.

Without their religious visions and voices, goes this explanatory approach, many women would be bereft of social influence. Women and other oppressed out-groups turn to religion and focus upon the next world because they do not have satisfying roles in this one; the oppressed need religious experience to give them roles and an arena for action. Women and slaves were eager converts to Christianity. Religious groups comprise one arena where women can gain attention and find self-expression. If women can claim experiences of invisible spirits, then their lower status can be remedied by relations with higher spiritual powers. Many female prophets, mediums and faith healers have found a devoted following that provide status and worldly rewards. A long line of women—from the Witch of Endor to the Delphic Sybil, to Mother Anne Lee, to Madame Blavatsky or Aimee Semple McPherson and countless modern New-Age channelers—have found a road to power and influence through spiritual influence.

A reductionist approach to religion that sees religious believers using their faith to gain social advantage follows the influential prophet of anti-Christianity, Friedrich Nietzsche. He preached that Christianity is the "most fatal seductive lie that has ever yet existed," and produces "despisers of life" who resent the strong and active who affirm life.[25] Slavish Christians resent the strong and powerful and create a religion that poisons society. And women in their weakness, along with other virtual slaves, will naturally be drawn to the comforting illusion that they will be rewarded with "pie in the sky when you die." Religion would be "the opium of the people," as Marx predicted. Marxists affirmed the thesis that humankind constructed religion and religious experiences in order to obtain consolation. In a harsh unjust social world religion provides an illusory escape for the downtrodden. Religion is scorned in leftist secular circles for the way it is used by powerful elites to keep the oppressed classes in submission.[26] Women and slaves and exploited workers can be pacified and persuaded to accept their lot because they are committed to Christian love, the necessity of suffering and general passivity. A constant stream of all of the various themes of doctrinaire antireligious atheism can be routinely found in the pages of the various magazines devoted to the crusade for secular humanism.

Many observers of the history of religion in American history have made the point that lower-class groups and minorities will be more likely to have spontaneous outbreaks of fervent and rapturous spiritual experiences.[27] Until the surprising advent of the modern charismatic movement within middle-class American Catholic and Episcopalian congregations, unrepressed emotional enthusiastic religious experience was mostly the domain of rural or storefront groups of poor, uneducated and often black congregants. Among educated churchgoers, openly expressed intense emotionalism was thought to be inauthentic if not neurotic. Again, hysterical women were thought to be the worst offenders. Obviously it is still the case that women who hear voices and see visions as part of their intense religious experiences present a challenge to both the theological and secular elites of academia. In the dogmatic materialism that reigns among many of America's intellectuals, there's no room for any reality beyond everyday "common sense" and whatever can be reasonably supported by empirical scientific evidence. Claims of being in communion with God will be routinely dismissed. The testimony of Christians, whether saints, mystics or ordinary devout women, can be lumped together with members of cults like Heaven's Gate or James Jones's followers. The extremity of Islamic fundamentalists and suicide bombers add fuel to the antireligious critique. Yes, of course such people may be sincere and believe in the reality of their subjective experiences and beliefs, but they can only be deluded. Some self-deception will arise from ignorance, suggestibility and misinterpretation of normal phenomena, and some illusions will be symptomatic of mental pathology.

In the eyes of the faithful, it is all too easy to see that devout materialists make their own leaps of faith from certain known effects of clinical mental pathology to generalized explanations that include all the inspiring voices, visions and spiritual experiences reported by the devout. Dogmatic doubts of all religious experience float about freely in the skeptical atmosphere of our times. Such skepticism and pervasive disbelief, with its unproved assumptions that science has disproved the validity of religious experience, makes it harder for spiritual seekers to find their way to faith. Convinced believers also can find themselves subject to attacks of self-doubt and questionings of their own religious experiences. I recognize the problem because I, too, at times find myself doubting the authenticity of my own faith experience. The challenge of women's religious experience does not remain an abstract problem for me.

An Autobiographical Confessional Note

Although I am an engaged and devoted Roman Catholic Christian (a grateful convert of almost fifty years), I am also a trained psychologist who endorses the scientific search for truth. As a Christian believer and a practicing intellectual, I do not wish to be self-deceived or mired in illusion. Science has been defined by the Nobel Prize winner, physicist Richard Feynman, as "not fooling oneself." Science's dedication to experimentation, testing and the methodical use of doubt are necessary for a productive search for findings that can stand up to time and further experience. So too, Christians can echo St. Augustine in his quest for truth, who attests that one thing he knows for sure is that he does not wish to be deceived. Hence Christians in search of truth will also be open to therapeutic doubt and the testing of our God-given powers of human reason. We think and probe so that what is true and good in accordance with God's will can be accepted and held fast. When we have intense religious experiences we should be ready to reflect upon them in a search for understanding.

In my own case I worry most about those social and psychological explanations that would have me projecting my own internal needs upon reality. O, Nietzsche, Marx, Freud and Darwin, you have left your barbs in this believer's mind! The accusation that religious experiences are neurotic wish fulfillment, a way to social influence or a means of escaping reality challenge me to self-examination. Have I as a woman used religion to compensate for my timid failures to be a more active agent in the world? Are my religious experiences a subtle form of self-deception or delusions serving selfish needs? I grant that my worries and doubts may be more intense than those of others. My self-questioning is surely related to both my history and my general intellectual commitment to reasonableness. Since feminist thought has given women intellectuals permission to examine the personal roots of their professional projects I feel free to give a brief account of the genesis of my own concerns over the relationship between religion and psychology.

I was brought up in a southern military family which, like many others, had secrets lurking beneath its sunny conviviality. As a bright and curious child I constantly spied upon the glamorous and kind adults who surrounded me. My sister and I were being reared with loving affection by a devoted single (widower?) father and told that we were motherless children. After acquiring a nice stepmother, I continued with my habitual eavesdropping on my parents' conversations. One night I overheard my parents talking about us and discovered that my own mother, whom I could barely remember, was not dead, but had become mentally ill and been hospitalized—permanently. After a messy divorce and her breakdown, her whereabouts had become an unmentionable secret. Naturally, my ten-year-old self was changed by that night's discovery. Ah, things may

31

not be as they seem; a skepticism about surface appearances affirmed by both religion and science. Perhaps this experience was the genesis of my intellectual quest for the really true, and surely my mother's fate began my interest in the mind, mental illness and women's experiences. By now, decades have past and my poor demented mother is ninety-two and still hospitalized with schizophrenia. I have visited her for fifty years but have been helpless to alleviate the destructive effects of this dreadfully debilitating disease.

More to the point, my mother's young-adult trajectory to psychotic breakdown had been marked by the advent of a fanatical religious fervor, complete with religious delusions. My science-worshiping father, who had repudiated his own strict Baptist and Presbyterian upbringing, saw my mother's turn to religion as a typical symptom of mental pathology. He was therefore most distressed when in adolescence I became fervently devoted to Christianity and joined a small Protestant church. While my childhood religious experiences of God's grace in the world had been faintly discouraged, my adolescent religious conversion was greeted with a strong negative reaction. In our social circles, it was considered odd and worrisome to be too intensely religious—or too intellectual. Anna Freud said that the typical adolescent defenses against the disturbing upsurges of instinct at puberty are "intellectualization" and "asceticism." True enough in my case. But I can attest that while these defenses may make you rather rigid, fanatical and a puritan, they can work to keep a girl out of trouble. No self-indulgence would be tolerated, from tobacco to alcohol to sex or academic underachievement. School and church were my delight and provided the reward of high achievement and a college scholarship.

During my years at Bryn Mawr College I pursued my serious Christian spiritual quest while getting a degree in English literature. The college had long left its affiliation with its Quaker founders, but nearby Quaker meetings offered me new spiritual experiences. The Friends introduced me to the power of silent meditation and to the importance of working for peace and social justice. I felt, however, a growing need for a more formal liturgical and sacramental expression of faith, along with a more articulated philosophical and metaphysical grounding for my Christian belief. I moved from the Quakers to a low Episcopal church to a higher Anglo-Catholic church and finally burst forth into the wide-open spaces of "here comes everybody" Roman Catholicism. To become a Catholic at Bryn Mawr in those days was a fairly rebellious move. I identified strongly with the spiritual journey of Dorothy Day. Like Dorothy and so many other converts, I had moved beyond my family and secular circle and experienced an outpouring of joy and gratitude in the church. During my

33

particular religious honeymoon of spiritual enthusiasm, I embarked upon the other great honeymoon experience.

My marriage to Daniel Callahan, an aspiring philosopher, brought me more happiness and the intellectual stimulation of living in Harvard's graduate student community. As fellow travelers of Dorothy Day's Catholic Worker movement, our graduate school poverty held few fears for us. We did not hesitate to throw ourselves into a long, challenging domestic commitment to childbearing combined with a religious intellectual vocation. In our fervor we enthusiastically coped with seven children in ten years, including the traumatic tragedy of a sudden infant death. During this time I was sustained and lifted up by many intense religious experiences, but I did not as yet engage in psychological analysis of religion.

Much later, after many career and family moves, with my husband's employment assured, I began a part-time writing career as a way to have intellectual stimulation while staying home. In a few more years as my children grew up, I was able to return to graduate school. By this time I was ready to confront inner questions and took my first psychology graduate courses. I had written books and articles on women, religious feminism, sexuality and family matters and felt that I needed to study human experience more deeply and systematically. Today, after more books, I can recognize that my circuitous path to a Ph.D. in social psychology and my commit-ment to Christianity and the intellectual life are manifestations of the central themes of my life. What could be more crucial or fascinating than exploring the relationship of the human mind and religious experience—especially women's religious experience? My intellectual projects have grown out of personal dilemmas, personal conflicts and the social pressures of the turbulent times we have lived through. The theological concerns and psy-chological questions that I have explored have always emerged from a bottom-up approach to lived experience.

In the '50s, the shocking constraints and biases toward women I encountered in and out of the church led me to attempt a synthesis of Christianity and feminism. I came to endorse women's public leadership roles as well as faithful commitments to marriage and family. I wrote on women's new work challenges and on the need for changing views of sexuality and sexual roles in the family. Working out these questions and proceed-ing deeper into psychological explorations, I arrived at the fundamental questions of conscience and moral development. I can recognize that my own moral development from adolescence onward has been grounded in religious faith. In my moral quest I have been inspired, comforted and strengthened by the joys of worship and prayer. Very intense awe-inspiring episodes in prayer have come occasionally, and in between I have been sustained by uplifting ordinary times of celebration and worship. I am grateful that God has supported me through many hardships and struggles. But in moments of self-doubt I have worried. Can my fervent religious episodes be the result of those inherited schizophrenic genes producing illusory experiences? Or I have also had the opposite reaction and blamed myself for being too rationally critical and distrustful. With all the gifts I have received, I have still hung back from more religious commitments. Have I been lukewarm out of selfishness under the cover of fear of madness? It is tempting to retreat into critical doubt and rigid self-control as a defense against God's demanding presence. I have always remembered the gospel description of those encountering Jesus: "He was too much for them." Did people turn away from Jesus because they, like so many of us modern folk, could not decide the question of whether their religious experiences with Christ were authentic and from God? Perhaps doubts are more intense for those who live in a hyperpsychological age pervaded by secular reductionist dismissals of belief. Was it easier to have confidence and certainty when saints lived in a world in which supernatural powers and direct communications with God were never questioned?

At this point I am intellectually and morally convinced of God's existence and God's loving care for humankind, but I also know that illusory religious experiences can exist. Even a convinced feeling of certainty is no absolute guarantee of validity. In the most extreme cases of religious delusions the mentally ill can have complete conviction in the reality of their voices and hallucinations. Indeed, most psychotic experiences are real to the individuals having them. And I can no longer give any credence to those romantic views of psychoses so popular in the '70s, which maintained that psychotic experience should be seen as an authentic spiritual journey into an alternate reality.[28] In these views psychotics are merely people who have been labeled as ill because they had the courage to assert that it is really mainstream normal society that is sick. The "crazy" person is right to rebel against the charade of conventional reality. Psychoses should be seen as spiritual breakthroughs rather than breakdowns.

Certain feminist writers have claimed that many women have been defined as mentally ill as part of a patriarchal strategy to tame rebellious women.[29] Putting women away in institutions takes care of the "inconvenient" or "troublesome" ones. Surely it is true that some women in the past were falsely labeled insane in order to legally incarcerate them. Such ploys could serve male designs for power, a new marriage or control of a woman's inheritance. In medieval times the containment and silencing of women could be effected by forcing women into the convent. Feminists have been correct to call attention to the fact that unconventional rebellious women are punished in subtle and not so subtle ways. Call to mind the defamation of Mary Magdalene. But male abuses of power should not be overgeneralized or used to deny the reality of mental illness. The mysterious madwoman in the attic who terrorized Jane Eyre has been too easily adopted as one example of some of the ways all women can be victimized by men and by medical diagnoses. Bertha, the imprisoned madwoman, turns out to be Mr. Rochester's cast-off wife from an earlier marriage contracted during a youthful sojourn in the West Indies. Thus, for some feminists, this discarded woman's murderous rage was not due to mental illness but was an understandable reaction that could characterize all rejected women exploited by male oppression.

While such a politicized approach to female madness can be tempting, (and it was certainly tempting to me with my family history), it does not stand up to the evidence. Schizophrenia, and for that matter Alzheimer's disease and other brain impairments are not just false labels used to further male interests or the power of the medical establishment. Mental illness is a tragedy and not a journey into an alternative spiritual world. Women's diagnoses of mental illness are not a weapon in society's war against women. I have spent too much time in the back wards of mental institutions and done too much psychological research to doubt the assertion that mental disease is like other diseases. Mental disease is a breakdown or malfunction of those cognitive and emotional capacities that have evolved in homo sapiens to enable individuals to function in their social and natural environments. Depression and schizophrenia are worldwide scourges that appear in every population. Yes, social conditions, stress and environmental effects will play a part in the onset and course of mental illness, just as they do in all diseases. The values of a specific culture may also make a difference in the ways a mentally impaired individual is treated, but social forces cannot be blamed for the origin of mental pathology. And alas, mental delusions and hallucinations often involve religious themes and claims to divine inspiration. God tells the mentally ill person to kill or torture a victim, or God's voice damns the individual to hell and commands self-mutilation or suicide.

At the opposite emotional pole of psychotic dysfunction, the mentally ill person who suffers from mania can have euphoric inspirations and also hear divine communications and commands. Such ecstasies and megalomanic delusions cause harm to self and others, because the individuals become so completely out of touch with reality that they cannot protect themselves or others. If you are certain that you are God or Jesus Christ or omnipotent, then everything is possible (such as defying gravity in attempted flight out of windows) and everything is permitted. "I am God" is the message left to the police by the Washington area sniper murdering a string of arbitrarily chosen victims. Those who have recovered from manic-depressive illness have testified to the difficulty of continuing to take the medication to control their disease since normality meant giving up their manic episodes of elation and power.

Clearly, one question for all observers and self-observers is how to tell the difference between pathologies and normal nondestructive thoughts and emotions. When does eccentricity or an extreme mood become harmful impairment? When does a practice become pathological? In psychiatry and psychology the decision about whether some experience is abnormal and harmful or is within the range of the culture's norm is called "differential diagnosis." In traditional Christian spiritual theory and practice, a decision about the authenticity and validity of religious experiences has been called "the discernment of spirits."[30] Obviously there is a complex relationship between the two kinds of practical judgments. And perhaps the prudential problem becomes most difficult for those persons who believe that religious experience can be authentic and should be trusted when it is valid. Unbelievers have fewer problems dismissing spiritual experiences; they are all delusional in their view. Confronting the complicated facts of mental functioning as both a religious believer and advocate of scientific psychology is a more demanding challenge.

My personal agenda in taking on this intellectual challenge is twofold. While respecting the scientific validity of modern psychiatry, social psychology and cognitive science, I would like to be able to demonstrate that the general and automatic suspiciousness of women's religious experiences as illusionary and inauthentic is mistaken. I contend that there is growing evidence that human beings are innately religious, innately capable of intense religious experience and that this is a normal and positive psychological capacity. While cases of mental illness can exhibit religious themes and content, authentic religious experiences exist and further the flourishing of humankind. Unfortunately religion, like every other important higher capacity of human beings (language, reason, sex, scientific or artistic creativity), can become skewed and corrupted, but it is on the whole beneficial. Women's religious experience, in particular, can be seen as providing positive insights and resources. Granted, much of current analyses of religion and religious experience is reductionist and often hostile, but this may be changing. Change and progress constantly appear in both science and theology, as well as in the dialogue between them.

Basically, the human sciences are not in an essentially adversarial position to religion. Instead, all intellectual inquiry can help the faithful to a fuller understanding and comprehension of God's ways with creation. As a Catholic intellectual I believe that it is possible to seek truth because the God of truth is one with the God-in-Christ revealed in the gospels. As Avery Dulles has written, God is "the author of faith and reason," and there can be no ultimate conflict.[31] Truth is one. Faith progresses in its endless efforts to understand the revelation of God's good news throughout history, just as reason and the sciences progress in their efforts toward understanding the universe and human beings. If Christ is the truth, the way and the life, he invites us to follow wisdom and appreciatively explore God's good creation. Growth in understanding will continue until the final day of the eschaton. While Christians follow an infinite, ineffable God of mystery, we also proclaim that the meaning of mystery does not preclude intellectual inquiry or reasoned reflection. In fact, the existence of God as the source of all reason, rationality and truth inspires human inquiry and the search for understanding. Mystery can be seen as the existence of "infinite intelligibility," containing an invitation to seek progress on the reasoned path to understanding—as far as possible. The theologian Nicholas Lash has spoken of "the endlessness of making sense" of gospel revelation.[32] Every generation must take up the task. If our faith is a living faith, it must live for us and speak to our cultural world and historical condition. In a scientific and psychological age this faith must engage the challenges of the evolving human sciences, as well as assimilating the ever new developments of theology. New theological currents and understandings will produce new questions and perspectives.

A fervent belief in God and the gospel proclaimed by the church in its traditional gift of faith, however, does not automatically solve the question of how persons come to psychologically experience their faith. What is needed is more exploration of the ways persons sense the presence of the Divine in their lives and what theological understandings explain the process. To do this it is necessary to focus first on the controversial concept of experience before tackling a description of religious experience. Fortunately, I think it is now possible to glimpse some emerging religion-friendly psychological understandings of religious experience. Finally, I will ask whether and how these explorations relate to women's religious experience. Have the great women saints as well as their more ordinary sisters in the pews some unique insights to give us from their religious experiences?

43

Experience

Before we look at religious experience we should confront the problem of the use of the concept of experience. *Experience* has been called the "weasel word" because it is so difficult to pin down its meaning.[33] Experience can be used to refer to an outside external or objective view of general or collective events as well as to subjective internal personal consciousness. Is experience going to refer to everything that has ever happened to a person or to a group? This usage could expand the meaning of experience to include the whole history of the universe since the big bang. To take such an objective outside description of experience would broaden the category too much to be useful in exploring the authenticity of human religious experience. I think it more fruitful to limit the use of the word *experience* to refer to those internal, subjective, self-conscious, self-aware episodes in individual lives. Of course, since we are dealing with rational self-interpreting human beings, one of the elements of their subjective experience will be thoughts, emotions and reflections about the meaning of their own experience! So too, since humans are such social creatures, much of internal individual experience will take place in interactions with others. All of these internal, subjective, consciously perceived dimensions of personal living in the world are what I am going to reference as experience. I recognize that a full understanding of reality will include both internal, subjective perspectives as well as outside, communal objective perspectives. Science and philosophy aim to take what has been called the generalized abstract "view from nowhere," or rather, the view from everywhere. An objective, external view of things should be able to garner a consensus from all observers. But even limiting an inquiry to subjective, conscious awareness presents problems.

What about those things that have happened to human beings that they cannot at present remember? Can something that once happened to a person and then been forgotten still count as part of their subjective human experience? Well, it depends. Human beings live in sequential time frames and in limited space with limited capacities to process information. Consequently, individuals can never at one point in time be simultaneously conscious of all that they know or have stored in memory. At this moment I am writing a sentence and concentrating on a set of ideas, oblivious to anything else I know. But in a few moments I may be engaged in another task—fixing the computer, cooking dinner, riding a bicycle and so on. As my conscious attention shifts I become aware of the many other things that I know. Events that were once consciously processed can be stored in memory, temporarily set aside and then later be brought to mind or enter consciousness, either voluntarily or involuntarily. So we should say that

45

anything in the past that can potentially be brought into consciousness should also count as an individual's experience. In this amended definition those forgotten past events or skills that I can have access to will count, but those things forever below the threshold of consciousness, such as the way the brain retrieves memories or activates the immune system, would not.

While human beings are alive, they are continually progressing through different cycles and levels of consciousness, from alert hyperawareness and awareness to daydreaming and the various stages of dreaming sleep.[34] It seems appropriate to count as experience only what is presently in awareness or those things that can potentially be brought into self-awareness. Aspects of perception, stored images, emotions, thoughts and some procedural skills can easily count as subjective experience, since explicit awareness and attention can be focused upon them. In quiet reflective states or in therapy, individuals can also become aware of things that they know but formerly did not notice. Implicit knowledge and implicit memory can become explicit and accessible. Human beings are often surprised, pleased or disturbed by what emerges into self-awareness and consciousness, as well as by what has been unnoticed or lapsed from mind. Ancient and modern therapeutic wisdom has always counseled "know thyself," because so much knowledge that is initially obscure to conscious awareness can later become conscious.

Yet there is no denying that much that has happened from conception onward in an individual life, including things happening in the present functioning of an individual, cannot be the focus of awareness or ever brought to mind. We float within a vast sea of unnoticed events and flows of information impinging upon us from outside and from internal workings of our brains and bodies. Outside events such as subtle climate changes or radiation effects or slow forces of evolution or social change will not be noticed, even if they do affect us as part of the general experience of humankind. Within the individual organism, humans do not have conscious access to brain processes, biochemical reactions, genetic expressions, organ functioning or immune and disease processes, among other things.

Also, there are aspects of human functioning, like breathing or blinking, that are usually nonconscious but can sometimes be consciously experienced. Memory, too, can be intentionally activated or can be spontaneous. Human organisms are composed of many different complex information-processing systems that affect and shape the individual's function in changing environments, but not all of the information processed and taken in ever becomes subjective conscious experience—and a good thing, too. Who could do anything else if a person had to consciously be in charge of the liver's or the kidneys' functioning? Then there are other learned activities that were once conscious and intentional, but when they become habitually automatic, almost drop from awareness. Once having learned complex skills, like driving or typing (or manners and morals?), they become second nature. They do not require the precious resources of conscious attention. Highly aware states of self-consciousness have to be used efficiently and appear to be reserved for special needs such as new learning, creative activities, making important decisions and long-term planning. Prayer and worship also require attention, although in great saints it, too, seems to become automatic.

Many of the arguments about human experience and the operation of human consciousness stem from different estimates of how self-awareness arises from nonconscious, unaware, automatic functions. How does implicit, nonconscious processing become explicit and conscious experience? Another perennial puzzle is how much individuals can control what goes on either internally, interpersonally or in the environment. Those who deny the freedom of the will or the human ability to make conscious choices that cause actual effects say that everything we think or feel we are choosing is really determined by nonconscious factors operating in the internal and external environment.

The most skeptical deterministic thinkers see self-consciousness or free will as part of the "folk psychology"—an illusion that helps people live together with the fiction of moral responsibility. Naturally, when free will is dismissed as illusory, it is particularly easy to dismiss religious experiences and religious behavior as well. But such radical reductionist views of human experience have not won the day in either science or philosophy.[35] Most people, including most scientists, are convinced that they do operate as conscious agents who are having and directing their experiences for much of their waking hours.

Emerging states of consciousness seem to be constantly moving and changing, and the process was aptly named by William James as "the stream of consciousness."[36] The stream is uneven (James uses the analogy of a bird that flies, perches for a while and then flies off again). Consciousness is also complex and qualitatively different, depending upon the variations in emotional coloring or the warmth from personal investment. Emotions and more focused logical processes arise, fade and operate in complex interactions with behavior, perception and physiological processes. The stream of experience has been compared to "a musical fugue," with different themes entering and leaving the score.[37] A spontaneous free-floating waking stream of experience, sometimes called daydreaming or musing, can take place and alternate with more focused task-oriented thinking. A normal unimpaired adult individual under ordinary circumstances (not in a threatening emergency) can direct and focus attention and choose to fix attention upon a task or a problem. The will and will power for reasoning, acting and creative imagining can be manifested in the ability to focus conscious attention despite distractions, and thereby control and shape our experience.

Persons seem to innately differ in this ability, but individuals can be educated and trained to direct and choose to hold their attention. Children learn to study, work and behave well by rejecting temptations and distractions. Educational programs and spiritual novitiates specialize in shaping the human ability to direct the focus of the conscious aware self. Through directed consciousness the human species has specialized in invention, problem solving, philosophical reasoning, art, morality and religion. The unique human ability to direct self-consciousness produces not only a creative mastery of the environment but also unique capacities for self-transformation.

The capabilities of consciousness can include paying attention to memories of past events, imagined events, planned scenarios for the future and vicarious participation in the narratives and experiences of others. Humankind is shaped by interpersonal interactions. All the groups to which an individual belongs will shape a person's ongoing experience through memory and past learning. Mutual words, actions and emotions produce a challenging stream of new information to be processed. From infancy to death, the self and self-awareness are shaped through the give and take of imagined or real interpersonal responses. The claim has been made that all individual conscious experience is actually collective in origin, although an individual can also interact with the nonpersonal environment and grow through engaging in difficult tasks. As psychologists have begun to explore optimal experience, conditions of "flow" have been investigated in which consciousness is engaged with a task that fully absorbs attention.[38] The challenge of the activity and the capacities of the subject are so matched that the absorbing positive experience allows time and any uncomfortable self-awareness of struggle to fade from consciousness. Paradoxically, in flow, the optimal engagement of the self's interactions with the other produces a kind of self-forgetfulness. One gains the self by losing it in active giving—and subsequently feels refreshed and renewed—a familiar idea in spirituality.

Religious Experience

Given the above definition of experience, we would say that religious experience is some aware, conscious participation in religious phenomena.

But what do we count as religious phenomena? Too broad a definition that takes in any form of heightened consciousness of value will become meaningless, and too narrow a definition also misses the mark. Certainly religious experience is made up of more than participation in organized religious institutions or in groups holding certain beliefs and doctrines in common. In or out of formal structured events, human beings are innately predisposed to have transcendent experiences and to be conscious of realities that go beyond the concrete here and now of daily life.[39] Human beings can sense, or imagine invisible nonpresent realities, including infinity. Infinity can be implicitly recognized, for instance, in the fact that language use is so open-ended that any sentence can go on forever, just by the addition of another clause. Conversations could continue without end. Numbers, too, can extend forever by adding one to any present quantity. From ancient times words and numbers have been seen as having a mystic eternal quality. So too, humans can be transported and carried away by the beauty of nature or the beauty of art and music. The emotions of love and joy, which soar and produce desires for eternal intimacy, also give human experiences of another realm beyond the prosaic. Emily Dickinson voices a universal human response when she writes,

This world is not conclusion;
A species stands beyond,
Invisible, as music,
But positive, as sound.

Human beings employ symbols and make art when or where the species appears. The use of flowers and red dye in ancient burial remains signals that the first humans could envision a reality beyond what is concretely present. Emotional awareness of mutual love and the giving and getting of joy in a beloved's presence also produces an experience of transcendence. The desire to live, love and enjoy others forever springs from the positive emotional aspects of human life together. Religion springs from the need to explain positive life experience as well as from any defensive moves against death. But the knowledge that death will end life's goodness intensifies the longings of the heart. The knowledge of intellectual and physical limits combined with the ability to imagine infinity and alternatives to what is present induces religious thoughts. Constraints and limits can incite the desire for infinite freedom and power. Surely, human participation in art, music, intellectual and scientific inquiry and human love manifest the human capacity for transcendent experiences. Religion, of course, fully manifests these urges and desires for an unending life of love, beauty and meaning beyond human limits and the struggle for survival. But transcendent experiences can exist without religion, as our secular age has proven. Aesthetic feelings, human love and intellectual seeking flourish among atheists and unbelievers. These elements are intimately related to religious experiences but are not the same in the secular realm.

In full-blown distinctly religious phenomena a supernatural or unseen "spiritual" dimension to reality is affirmed.[40] Thus religious experience must go beyond other transcendent human experiences in an explicit affirmation of the existence of unseen realities beyond ordinary life. William James describes religious experience as an affirmation and contact with the invisible More that surrounds all ordinary visible waking life. And the More is held to be the supremely important grounding for this life. The suprasensible or supernatural realm transcends nature and explains all existence. Accompanying the religious awareness of the beyond or deeper reality is the felt human need to get one's incomplete, limited, unworthy self into right relation with the ultimate ground of all things. Humans sense that they are incomplete, or not whole or holy, and believe that through religion they can be healed. In seeking to know the More and seeking to be healed, humans have engendered a variety of religions.

Today, highly elaborate world religions have developed sprawling complexes and well-wrought systems of ongoing institutions, theological doctrines, sacred scriptures and prescribed practices of worship, prayer, meditation and contemplation. For James, the criteria for judging any religion is not so much its institutional development, its origins or the personality of its founding geniuses, but whether on the whole the religion is philosophically reasonable, morally helpful and provides immediately luminous experiences. Most high religions will include systems of meaning, mandates for moral and ethical behavior and ways to induce feelings of direct participation in realities beyond the visible and concrete world. Religion can give humankind a sense of direct contact and communion with God or the ultimate ground of reality through prayer, meditation and worship. Sensing God's presence and even receiving revelations of and from God can be a central part of religious experience. The cognitive beliefs and ethical mandates of a religion are infused with emotional energy and passionate investment because of the sensed presence of God. Adoration, praise and joy are an integral part of religious experience. A typical instance from the Christian tradition rings out daily around the world in Mary the Daughter of Zion's cry, "My soul magnifies the Lord and my spirit rejoices in God my savior." The beginning of the Magnificat celebrates God's goodness and is followed by a recognition of God's accomplishment of a just ordering of this world. To fuse a sense of the supernatural divine presence with the moral mandate for just behavior is part of the religious genius of a high universal religion. The worship of the numinous Holy One who transcends all ordinary reality is fused with the demand for everyday goodness to one's neighbor in some formulation of the golden rule. The intellectual, the moral and the spiritual aspects of religion are fused. Christians, like the Jews, take part in individual and communal worship and praise, as well as striving to carry out God's will for justice in every aspect of their lives.

William James, for all of his genius, also had blind spots in his approach to religious experience.[41] In addition to his worries about effeminacy, James did not much understand or resonate with the communal dimension of religions. This led him to underestimate the positive contributions of collective institutions in transmitting religious beliefs. It is the group that enacts the communal liturgies and rituals of worship that most reliably produce numinous experiences in each new generation. James had been imprinted from youth with his family's strong individualistic American Protestant heritage and puritan sensibilities. There is no resonance in James with the Catholic belief in the church as sacrament, or its continuing existence as the mystical body of Christ through time. The idea that we encounter Christ in the church and in communion with one another in common worship is foreign to

James, who thought of institutionalized religion as an obstacle to authentic firsthand inward religious experience of God in solitude. The charismatic religious individual will be thwarted by the group's tendency toward conventional static external forms of belief. James thought of mystic illumination and inward conversion as happening within the individual heart and mind. He agreed that true religious experiences would have to increase love and charity toward others, but the inspiration comes from within. James does not seem to be vividly aware of Christ's promise that "where two or three are gathered in my name, I am there among them" (Matt 18:20). Psychology's explorations of group dynamics and group synergy played little part in his approach to religious experience.

Another influential explorer of religious experience following James in the 1920s was Rudolf Otto, with his famous book *The Idea of the Holy*.[42] Otto, like James, stresses the importance of the individual's emotional numinous feelings in religious experience. Emotions give life and color to the cognitive religious beliefs that a person holds. Individuals sense an overwhelming mysterious reality beyond them, and they respond with feelings of creaturehood and dependence. For Otto, awe and a fascination verging on dread and fear are innate responses to the Holy. A sacred all-powerful overwhelming reality can be sensed by human creatures. In what Otto calls the "mysterium tremendum," the sacred and ineffable mystery is felt to possess all the energy, power and plenitude that a human creature lacks. Humans are fascinated at the same time that they feel dread before the Holy One who possesses all power and goodness. While the Holy includes the moral and ethical dimensions of reality, it cannot be reduced to the good or to the merely moral. Otto describes the worshiper encountering the Sacred Other and feeling terror, wonder and awe. A sense of unworthiness is induced in the creature before such an overwhelming Reality. What Otto describes as unique to the religious experience certainly applies to the Old Testament accounts of the people's dealings with the Yahweh of fire and thunder. Otto's descriptions of religious experience seem biased toward male imagery; he ignores images of God as Mother as well as the mystical experience of women.

Otto also seems to slight those experiences of transcendence available to all humankind outside of the religious sense of the Holy. I would demur from his claim that a sense of awe and creaturely dependence is the product of a special religious faculty rather than arising from the whole of human capacities. As we understand the complexities of cognitive consciousness and the strength, subtlety and range of human emotions, the religious emotions described by Otto do not require specific mental equipment. The evolved human brain operates as a whole in religious responses.

Awe before great power can be a secular human response to nature and human events. Looking at war, thinking about the Holocaust or contemplating the scientific findings of cosmology, evolution or physics can create a feeling of fascinated terror. Dread can accompany the fear of annihilation from nuclear explosions and induce in unbelievers a sense of how little they can control the powers surrounding them. Secular agnostics can sense the overwhelming mysteries of the universe without feeling they have encountered their Creator. In this same way, the joyful exaltations that art, music and love induce are not prominent in Otto's description of knowing God. The innate and natural human experiences of transcendence may be more pervasive than Otto thinks. Intense emotions can penetrate and accompany all thinking and consciousness, not just religious experience.

A contemporary instance of a broader and more inclusive analysis of religious experience can be found in the work of Rodney Stark, an eminent sociologist of religion. He attempts to draw up a taxonomy of religious experiences that echoes earlier thinkers such as James and Otto. Stark also thinks that the essential element of religious experience "which distinguishes it from all other human experience is *some sense of contact with a supernatural agency.*"[43] The contact in itself, however, is not conceived to be as intense a human capacity as Otto asserts, for it is not always overwhelming.

Stark asserts that different kinds and degrees of contact are possible, because he conceives the encounter as though it were an interaction or communication between two actors. Interactions can differ in degree and kind, but the contact, however slight, will be experienced as contact with some divine essence or ultimate reality. Transcendental authority is usually named as God, and God is thought of as a supernatural actor. To count as religious experience the individual or the group must perceive, define it as such and consciously see the experience as supernatural.

A person or group can be seen to engage in four possible configurations of inter-actor relations on a continuum of closeness and intimacy. The different degrees can be seen as: "(1)The human actor simply notes (feels, senses, and so on) the existence or presence of the divine actor;(2)Mutual presence is acknowledged; the divine actor is perceived as noting the presence of the human actor; (3)The awareness of mutual presence is replaced by an affective relationship akin to love or friendship; (4) The human actor perceives himself or herself as a confidant of or as a fellow participant in action with the divine actor."[44] In other words there is a continuum of intimacy from bystander to acquaintanceship to friendship to intimate communion and cooperation. Different people may have different religious experiences at different times, but the more intimate intense very complex relationships will characterize the mystics. While feelings and emotional states of love and friendship may be common, the presence of visions, voices and trances will be rare. Stark's categories for describing the variety of religious experiences are intriguing and adequate for most religions, although I am not sure they work so well for some forms of Buddhism that do not affirm a divine personal agent. But the taxonomy is appropriate for Roman Catholic Christianity, with its concept of a personal God seeking to communicate with creatures and bring them into union with the Trinity. Also, throughout church history Christians have reported the different degrees of awareness and intimacy with God that Stark has described.

Stark further analyzes the continuum of religious experiences into the confirming experience, the responsive experience, the ecstatic experience and the revelational experience. The revelational experience will be challenging to believers because of its cognitive content. In this form of religious experience, persons receive divine messages and commands that are to be applied to the world and its inhabitants. For Stark, visions and voices can accompany confirming and ecstatic experiences and convey special unique messages and information to a person. Other revelational religious experiences can convey messages through signs and symbols, "but typically revelations are spoken." The messages can be prophetic or theological, a commissioning of a particular action or some combination of the above. Some messages are quite orthodox in that they do not deviate from the particular religious communion's view of things, but some are heterodox and take issue with the prevailing understandings of God's will. The latter of course present the greatest problem for observers. If a revelation is only concerned with an individual believer's personal journey to holiness, that is not disturbing. But if the voices command the visionary to recruit an army or conquer a city, that is different. A prophetic revelation that condemns some established practice or commands some new form of worship also presents a challenge to existing religious communities. Then the problem of discerning an experience as authentic rather than spurious or pathological becomes intense. One astute investigator of the social psychology of religion puts it this way: "As one goes from confirming to revelational expressions, the probability of serious reality disturbances involving delusions and hallucinations seem to increase."[45] All believers would realize that there is a problem when psychology tries to trump and pass judgment on religion, but all believers should also admit to the caution that "even religious traditions do not define their adherents as immune to mental disorder."[46] With this question one is back to the interaction between "differential diagnosis" and the "discernment of spirits." And back to hysterical women.

The problem of discerning what is going on in some unusual encounter can be intensified if the reported religious experience of a supernatural agent involves evil. Stark affirms that people can report a continuum of awareness and communication with diabolical and evil supernatural spirits, ranging all the way from uncanny uneasiness to terrorizing to diabolic possession. Whether on the positive or negative continuum, Stark thinks that persons may progress from simple awareness to greater closeness. With evil, the move is from temptation to cooperation to diabolic possession. But when the movement is in the positive direction toward a good God, people report an emotional sense of joy that becomes more and more intense. One moves from the "something there" of quickened warmth to the intimate healing saving fiery hot ecstatic union that in some cases can engulf ordinary consciousness. These transient trances and exalted states of benevolent possession are common in many cults and also occur in Christianity. These extreme ecstatic states of swooning have been called being "slain in the spirit," or being "caught up in the spirit." Not surprisingly, analogies to the ecstasy of sexual orgasm have been used to describe the temporary and ecstatic loss of consciousness that accompanies overwhelming unions of joy that confirm and refresh worshipers.

As we have seen, intense religious experiences often induce strong hostility and disparagement from secular skeptics. Unbelievers see more pathology or self-deceptive illusions when God is seen as playing an active role in communing with a human being. Everyone can grant the acceptability of mildly confirming feelings of transcendence and benevolence, because these feelings are so akin to universal experiences of human love or aesthetic responses to music and art. Peak experiences of happiness and oneness with nature are everywhere described in literature and artistic creations. Atheists may be unable to explain the presence of transcendent experiences within a meaningless accidental universe, but they do not deny human responses to love and beauty. But when God is considered to be personal and acts in history to communicate with believers, especially to uneducated women and children, then doubt and skepticism arise to a full-force gale. Yearnings from humankind to the universe in general can be accepted as real, but skeptics refuse to grant that a personal God speaks to humans.

For their part, even believing Christians have difficulties understanding the theological and intellectual foundations informing the claim that God is the source and origin of valid and authentic religious experience. Here too, the more intense and unusual religious experiences such as hearing voices and seeing visions present the most problems. Two challenging questions must be answered. One question involves the existence of inauthentic mistaken religious experiences or voices that undeniably appear in mental pathologies. "God told me to kill my child who is a devil," or "God told me to mutilate myself." Why and how can these inauthentic inspirations exist side by side with God's true revelations? And in authentic religious experiences exactly how does God communicate with humankind?

Both of these questions concern the way God relates to creation and to God's human creatures—a very old theological issue. Today the questions have become more complex because of our new understandings of the human mind/brain/body unity and the mystery of the operation of human consciousness. When a Christian "hears" the voice of God or is "prompted" by the Spirit or receives revelations, consolations or joyous spiritual experiences, exactly what in God's name is happening? In a sense the believer has more of a challenge comprehending the possibility of both authentic and invalid religious experience than the secular skeptic who can summarily dismiss all religious experience as self-created illusions of misguided or neurotic individuals. A Christian who believes in authentic religious experiences of God and at the same time admits that illusory mental pathologies also exist is saddled with the question of how to tell the difference between them as well as the question of how this all works together theologically. How do we understand God's operations in this conundrum?

Tentative Approaches to a Catholic Theological Framework for Religious Experience in Accord with Psychological Evidence

Christians today confront the question of religious experience within an ever more dynamic theological story of God and creation. God can now be understood to work through time and through evolution in such wondrously subtle ways that older static views of the world and revelation have to be discarded. The Roman Catholic Church has listened to its scripture scholars and theologians and moved away from the constraints of a literal, fundamentalist reading of its sacred texts and inspired traditions. Today all Catholic theologians repudiate biblical fundamentalism and recognize that scripture must be interpreted in all its complexity. These interpretations start with a plain literal sense of the words but are enriched by allegorical, analogical, mystical and moral readings. The different senses of scripture, of course, have been recognized since the time of the church fathers, but today interpreters have a more expansive array of new tools arising from knowledge of ancient archeology, anthropology, history, socio-cultural conditions, linguistic analyses, literary form, source criticism and so on. A scriptural narrative of a religious experience or of a revelatory communication from God can have many layers of meaning that can be gleaned from different kinds of textual, contextual and cultural analysis. Theologically, however, the whole is greater than the parts, and believing Christians affirm that each part of inspired scripture, or each story included in the canon, must be understood within the revelation of the whole gospel message. For Roman Catholics the whole gospel message is communicated through reading scripture within the church's Spirit-inspired communal understanding of God's revelation. As the church progresses through time and history to the final day of fulfillment in the eschaton, more and more understanding and fuller interpretation of God's good news can be comprehended.

In the same way, the tradition of church pronouncements and teachings cannot be read in an exclusively literal or static way. The development of tradition is now receiving the kind of attentive theological analysis that the different senses of scriptural interpretation has received. Tradition in the church includes much more than the formal pronouncements, since a whole Christian way of life or a whole community's religious experience is being reproduced in each new generation. These new dynamic interpretations of tradition can be seen in a work such as *Senses of Tradition: Continuity and Development in Catholic Faith* by theologian John

E. Thiel.[47] Thiel argues that Roman Catholic theology can claim an enlarged, more subtle understanding of the different ways of interpreting tradition. Thiel claims that Catholic theology, unlike certain forms of Protestant thought, does not collapse tradition into scripture. Both scripture and tradition have their own role in revealing God's truth. Tradition as a source of revelation functioned prior to the formation of the scriptural canon and has continued as a ground and source for understanding God's revelation. Tradition, taken in its plain, literal sense, includes all the formal written decrees of councils, encyclicals and so on, but tradition also includes all of those practices and beliefs that have been constantly handed down in the universal church. So, in addition to the literal sense of interpretation, Thiel describes three other senses, or ways to interpret tradition.

One sense is a "development-in-continuity" interpretation, in which it can be seen that doctrines gradually change as they are being newly appropriated by each generation. (This constant reappropriation of memory of the past seems to give meaning to Paul Ricoeur's wonderful phrase "the neo-past.") Two other dynamic developmental aspects of tradition give an understanding of how change and renewal take place in the church. Thiel describes a sense of tradition that he labels "dramatic development," which includes discontinuity and reversals at a point in history. In the teachings of Vatican II, for instance, certain magisterial teachings that were firmly entrenched for several centuries were set aside and subsumed into newer understandings. Doctrines disallowing religious liberty of conscience in a state or declarations that outside the Roman Catholic Church there is no salvation are now gone. They are seen as inadequate understandings of what God intends for humankind.

Another intriguing sense of tradition described by Thiel reveals the way an "incipient," "anticipatory" sense of development leads to renewal in the future. This recognition of anticipatory tradition is important in understanding women's religious experience. In a vital, ongoing church communion striving to become ever more attuned to Christ and the Holy Spirit, new and different insights into God's will can emerge in some local group within the church. While at the beginning these insights and practices seem revolutionary, they anticipate the future development of the teaching of the whole church. Some minority among the faithful, often living and working at the margins of the mainstream, may produce a novel and contested interpretation of church tradition. Gradually, however, the new prophetic perspective spreads, moves to the center and becomes assimilated into the universal church's consensus of the faithful to be proclaimed. The importance of the liberty of individual conscience, the rejection of slavery and the acceptance of women's social equality began as minority views, and so did the positive attitudes toward the Jews and other religions. Theologians like Thiel affirm that God's activity in the Holy Spirit manifests a dynamic complex plural movement through time and history. Accepting dynamic movement and change in the church's understanding of the gospel gives testimony that God's ever creative Spirit pours forth living waters. Novelty and change are signs of fruitfulness. While all interpretations of tradition may yearn for the Spirit's One Truth in a coherent, finally understood unity, Christians should not pretend to possess an abstract timeless completed order that is false to the reality of God's dynamic ways of interacting through history with God's creation. Both constancy and the change of renewal are necessary in religious experience. The canons of scripture and tradition that become universal constants and allow the reception of God's true word do so because they reflect the continuing lived assent of the Spirit working within generations of the faithful. Christian truth should not be thought of as an inert lumpen deposit confined to the past, but is more like a rich multithematic symphony playing through time into God's future. God as our future draws us on. More is coming and more can be expected. This dynamic approach to God's continuing creation validates the idea that God can be speaking to us and communicating in the present with the creation and creatures.

Such ideas of dynamic development through time into the future echo current evolutionary understandings of the universe. In evolutionary processes, stability and gradual continuous change are complemented by sudden discontinuities, extinctions and mutations that allow new species to appear and dominate an environment. In nature, as in religious and cultural development, a certain amount of disorder and chaos is necessary to facilitate novelty and to allow development. Roman Catholic theologians are responsive to evolutionary findings because the faithful trying to understand God's ways with creation will use all the scholarly resources of discovery at their command.[48] Scientific and cultural discoveries inevitably influence religious understandings. As one Jesuit theologian who works at the Vatican puts it, "...in appealing to our experience of God's action in the world we must appeal to the full range of that experience, including what is given us by the natural sciences."[49] And included in this exploration of the fullness of known human experience will be the human and social sciences.

Taking God's creation and evolution seriously, Christians can no longer ignore psychological inquiries into human consciousness or the indubitable evidence of the unity of body, brain and mind.[50] The psychology of religious experience cannot regress to a static dualistic worldview in which a strict separation between the natural and the supernatural world gave us the ghost in the machine. Once the incarnation is accepted as God's entrance into embodied history, a new unified approach is necessary. With more sophistication about the way ancient philosophies influenced early Christianity, theologians can see that much of the tradition was constricted by ancient Greek understandings that perfection required immutability and unchanging self-sufficiency. But for us, God's perfection and creativity is manifest in creative change and the ever new. "Behold I make all things new." God as a fountain of creativity is bringing a new creation into being through time and history into the future.

Creation can now be understood as open and evolving in freedom. Just as truth is not a lumpen deposit, neither is the dynamic universe, which is in process of becoming. God works in cocreative ways with human beings and within nature. Chance and necessity have both been created by God and operate in creation as God's way to bring about novelty and freedom.[51] Freedom and chance are necessary for creatures to have the autonomy to make choices, to create and to voluntarily seek to become friends and adorers of God. Thus God self-limits divine power and gives Godself totally to the creation just as Jesus the Christ humbled himself as a slave to give his all for humankind.[52]

God as Love gives up coercive dominion for the sake of giving creatures and creation freedom to become. God does not coerce creatures, but rather creatively persuades, attracts and draws creatures onward, upward and inward into God's future. God's complete self-giving and commitment to humankind, in becoming fully human in the incarnation, are the measure of God's loving gift. True lovers delight in the difference of the other and desire their development in freedom. As the theologian Nicholas Lash puts it, "All things exist as expressions of God's knowledge and God's love; as finite refractions of the absolute relations—eternal utterance, inexhaustible donation—that God is."[53] As God eternally utters the Word and in love gives the life of giving or donation within the Trinity, so God relates to the world and creation.

Today there has been a theological reclaiming of understandings of God as Trinity and the role of the Holy Spirit. The Holy Spirit can no longer be described as "the forgotten God."[54] Christians remember more fully that the Holy Spirit is the eternal donation or life-giving relationship within God, and so inspires, comforts, counsels, guides, enlightens and empowers individual believers and the church as an embodied communion living through history. One God, as Trinity, exists in mutual giving and receiving of love in community. Christ is God made visible as God's Word. God as ineffable Creator dwelling in unapproachable light is too distant for us to see. God as Holy Spirit sustaining and creating all things within the creation is, like air, too close and immanent for us to see. But we can see Christ and the fruits and gifts of the Spirit. In the Spirit human beings are transformed and enabled to be creative in good works.

Christian theologians proclaim that when Christians understand the Trinity they can know that the ultimate Reality is loving, mutual relationship. Rather than thinking of God as a distant, self-sufficient, omnipotent sovereign judging all, demanding a placating sacrifice and exacting obedience, a loving God is proclaimed who "affects all and is affected by all."[55] God sustains the creation and is constantly creating, attracting and inspiring all. Theologians speak of God as "the Wellspring of novelty," "the Fountain of creativity," "our absolute Future," and see "the divine Liveliness" bringing about God's Beauty. A God who gives Godself to the creation and refuses to coerce can be seen as God as Risktaker, God as Weaver, God as a musical Improviser, bringing a new creation to birth.[56] In efforts to understand the complete giving of Love, as modeled in Christ, theologians can speak of "the humility of God" and "the empathy of God."[57] God can be seen as complex and dipolar, because God is both transcendent and immanent.[58] God is eternal and faithful in steadfastly birthing the new creation. The struggle of bringing the new creation to birth in freedom can result in suffering, such as the experience of the cross as lived by Christ. Since the universe and creatures are free, suffering comes from its incompleteness and refractoriness. Chance operates as well as necessity, and freedom means that evil can come from evil choice or evil chance. God's invitation to love and relationship can be refused and sin and evil exist despite God's will for benevolence and harmony.

A dynamic and relational understanding of a creative God of love who gives totally and renounces coercion has profound implications for human religious experience. As noted above, God desires communication and communion, and wills to be accessible. But since the new creation is as yet unfinished and struggling to be born in God-given freedom, human errors and evil exist. The freedom and chance that allow novelty and human cooperation in creation also allow for mistakes, disasters, death and mental and physical diseases. Benevolence, beauty, order and lawfulness interact with chance, sin and evil. The evolved human mind's wondrous operations producing reliable knowledge can be seen as God-given but is also known to be limited and subject to pathology. Mentally ill persons who hear voices they identify as God persecuting them or commanding them to commit murderous acts are suffering from the diseases that arise in the flawed story of the world. Everything that happens is not directly willed by God and should not be accepted as part of God's immutable plan. God does not send earthquakes or cancer or schizophrenia, although an open evolving creation can include them. However, the freedom and openness of the creation leaves room for God's novel and creative actions everywhere as well as within human consciousness. After some evil or after some disaster God can creatively empower human beings to bring about the next best outcomes within time and history. There is no unfolding blueprint, so there can be many divine plans, depending upon the free responses of creatures. The fact that God's creative comforting powers help nurture persons facing evil or the aftermath of disasters has led the faithful to conclude that God intended the event beforehand. "God sent me cancer so that I would appreciate my family," and so on. Yet when Jesus healed the blind man, he seemed to state clearly that neither God nor the individual (nor the blind man's parents) had caused the disease, only that the disease was an opportunity to disclose God's mercy and healing powers. Christ's disciples, too, are commanded to heal all wounds but should not attribute their cause to God.

In accepting theological affirmations of God's love and gift of freedom in an open universe, it becomes clear that individual religious experience is important. Disciples will need communication with God to discern what to do in different situations. God's mandate to humans to be cocreators and act to bring about the new creation may entail embarking on novel enterprises. Recognizing that freedom and openness and the creation of chance may also bring about evils and pathologies, the need to understand human functioning is intensified. Can the unhealthy and incomplete elements of religious experience be discerned and confronted? William James had no problem admitting that many saints could be neurotic and have neurotic elements in their religious experiences, but still produce valuable religious insights. As noted, James insisted that judgments of the value of religious teachings and insights should be separated from considerations of the origins of the experience. And James also uses the traditional criteria of whether religious experience produces charity and virtue.

From New Testament times through all later approaches to spirituality, the testing and discernment of religious experience has relied on the rule that by their fruits you shall know them.[59] Does a religious experience increase love, strengthen virtuous behavior, increase reverence for God, Christ and scripture, move toward truth and goodness and away from evil? No recommendation for using evil means to obtain good could come from a good God. Any message that is domineering, blackmailing, or requires a person to engage in immoral activity could be from the Holy Spirit. Testing all things in order to hold fast what is good and true has been necessary from the beginning of the church, as a reading of scripture reveals. Or perhaps it is more accurate to say that after testing, a Christian should hold fast to the fruitful and true elements in a particular religious experience. As with the development of tradition and interpretation of scripture, new, fuller understandings can replace incomplete understandings.

Since, in God's creation, life is characterized by freedom but sustained through love and relationship, there will always exist an admixture, fusion and cooperation of the human spirit and the Holy Spirit. Scripture is fully human as well as inspired, and religious experience can also be fully human as well as infused with God's presence. An individual's religious experience of God's will and presence will be embodied in an individual's own language, thought forms and cultural references. God speaks everyone's native language. Always and everywhere, God knows, attracts and moves the human heart. But limited human beings given to sin and error and living in a flawed environment can misunderstand God's message. Even when there is no pathology or impairment or skewed mental processes there can be mistaken insights and mistaken prophecies, while at the same time God's Spirit communicates and discloses creative novel understandings of God to human beings. Such mistakes must arise since humans are limited and free to cooperate or not. God never coerces. Inspiration is not mental rape.

Even the most intense religious raptures that temporarily overwhelm everyday consciousness are felt as restorative. This demonstrates another tried and true way to judge a mystical religious experience. Does it make persons healthier and more energized as well as more loving and virtuous?

God in Christ steadfastly invites everyone into love, truth and life. Christ stands at every door and knocks. The love offered is the same in the most intense relationships with fervent disciples as with the less favored or with the lost sheep. But the fire that dramatically flames forth in some hearts can also burn quietly. (Embers, too, may still exist among unbelievers.) There is one Spirit who acts in the world and ardently courts the hearts and minds of humankind, despite the differences of culture and individual temperaments. Those persons whose functions are mentally impaired and malfunctioning are no less loved. God relies on the gifts of disciples to be able to test all messages and experiences and discern the good.

Karl Rahner, the great twentieth-century theologian, confirms that religious experience is God-given but also must be tested. In his monograph on visions and prophecies, Rahner defends the truth that a creative God of love can and will reveal Godself to human beings, while recognizing that many mistakes can also be made.[60] Rahner is psychologically knowledgeable and familiar with the ways that pathological mental illness can produce voices and hallucinations that are clearly harmful and destructive. Sometimes, too, outright fabrications and frauds can take place in order to gain power or money. But visions and voices that are neither fabrications nor pathological symptoms of mental illness can also be filled with mistaken content. Sincere self-deception and error are possible. Because of the potential for error and self-deception, private religious experience, especially that of women, has often been suspect. When a private religious experience is prophetic and demands some response from others in the church, then the problem of critical discernment is intensified. Thus the universal church has often been slow to affirm that a prophecy or vision *may* be believed. "May," because only those truly canonical or fully tested consensual creedal proclamations of the Christian faith *must* be believed by Roman Catholics.

Rahner points out that many private visions and prophecies often contain theological inconsistencies with the received creeds and doctrines of the faith. Moreover, visionaries can contradict one another and make predictions that do not come true. These problems of authenticity remain even if and when good effects follow from the faith of devotees. Rahner, for instance, seems quite doubtful of the authenticity of the Fatima visions. He thinks that pious credulity and enthusiasm can lead believers to avoid the necessary critical testing of the reported facts as well as to bypass adequate theological analysis. Even when no fraud is in question, the problem of self-deception remains. As he says, "God does not deceive man, but man deceives himself."[61]

Yet despite the problems of discerning error, Rahner gives a positive assessment of private religious experience as a potentially valid and worthy work of the Holy Spirit building up the church. Rahner affirms the power and freedom of God to communicate with humankind at any time and place through any mode. In principle God as God the Creator can make Godself known through God's works and by his free personal word. Naturally every mode of communication that is employed by God will be conditioned by the historical time and audience in which it occurs. Moreover, individual religious experience can be oriented beyond the individual path to holiness and be prophetic for the whole church in its historical journey. In other words, Rahner defends the doctrine that prophecy can continue into postapostolic times. Much suspicion of private prophetic religious experience grew out of the belief that after Christ's full and final revelation of God, there could be nothing more for Christians to learn or hear. Some Christian thinkers have asserted that after apostolic times and the closing of the scriptural canon, no new communications or inspirations from God to the church would be received.

In this static backward-looking view, the Spirit would only safeguard the deposit of faith. But Rahner, who was familiar with scientific acceptance of evolutionary theory and affirmed God's complete self-giving (or kenosis) to the creation, contends that the Spirit continues to inform and inspire individuals in a dynamic future-oriented church. While Christ is God made visible and has given the final and full revelation of God, the kingdom's coming through history remains to be worked out. I always remember that Christ told his disciples that they would be called to do greater work than he, while Paul sees the whole creation groaning in birth pangs on the way to its final fulfillment, when God will be all in all. These concepts of unfinished work and an incomplete creation have now been emphasized by evolutionary theologians. But Rahner, writing in the early '60s, already makes the point that many evolving developments of the church will require new decisions suitable for new and different times and conditions. Thus he champions the importance of the private prophetic insights of believers that cannot "be replaced by hierarchy, or a mysticism of contemplation devoid of images."[62] The religious experience of individuals cannot be subsumed by any other church role or office. The Spirit acts to build up the church in many ways and uses different gifts to guide the path of the ever reforming church. The institutional hierarchical functions of the church cannot operate alone.

Often too, Rahner notes, visions and communications through individual religious experience will reinforce what is recognized as worthy and needful to be done. Inspirations will serve to energize the action of the faithful, and can be thought of as ways that the Spirit can give psychological help to the church. Interestingly enough, Rahner notes that "It is a striking circumstance that this function has been exercised in recent times exclusively by women."[63] Christian feminists would not see this as a surprise, since women have been barred from holding hierarchical office. Fortunately, the Spirit has always blown where it will and in all places and times communicated new life to all, often through women's experience. If we go back to John Thiel's analysis of the way tradition can develop in "anticipatory" or "incipient" ways, it can be seen that new insights for the future development of the church will often come by the work of the Spirit among minorities excluded from the mainstream.

The private religious experiences of women barred from hierarchical authority can be affirmed as a rich source of strength for the church as a whole with an anticipatory thrust in the midst of continuity. When something new is proposed it will be tested to see if it is consonant or in harmony with God's word and revelation, or perhaps completes them in some way. Despite the presence of errors, deceptions, self-deceptions and the presence of fakes and frauds, Rahner theologically validates the value of individual religious experience. At the same time he reiterates the need for prudent discriminations and discernment about the authenticity of religious experience.

Yet accepting the traditional criteria for discerning whether the promptings and various kinds of religious experience are from God does not explain how these ideas, feelings, images and voices arise within human consciousness. William James confirmed the tradition's advocacy of testing religious experience by criteria of value, virtue, charity and fruitfulness, but he also wanted to understand how religious experiences emerge. Should it not help us to make more informed discernments if we could understand more about human consciousness and the psychology of religious experience?

Religious experience arises within the operations of human consciousness, but here we meet a formidable obstacle. No one in either science or theology understands how human consciousness emerges or operates. Fitting together the incompletely understood pieces of the psychological brain/mind puzzle with the mystery of God's inspiration is a formidable challenge. Wrestling with the difficulties presented by understanding how human consciousness arises from the brain is going to continue for many years, if it can ever be resolved. Some secular thinkers, sometimes called "mysterians," have thought that it will be impossible for humans to do so since the brain is the product of evolutionary forces that are larger than itself. Could a dog understand Einstein's theory of relativity? Maybe not, but humans have been created to seek knowledge and understanding, and at least lessen the amount of ignorance that exists. At this point in my attempts to comprehend the interaction of psychological knowledge and theological understanding, I am helped by two analogies. Drawing on theological and scientific understandings, we can seek to envision how human beings can have authentic religious experiences of God and yet be subject to error.

The Human Being as a Living Information Receptor

In a first analogy we can instructively look to the natural world, which is permeated with information and omnipresent invisible signals. With the proper receptors invisible messages, images and sounds that convey meaning coming from the surrounding environment can be received on radios, televisions, telephones, radars and other monitoring devices. At times, however, the informational signals cannot get through to a receiver because of environmental barriers or other "noise" that gets in the way. The interference may be caused by storms or power failures, or the receptor itself may be broken or defective to some degree. My fancy is that the brains of human beings should be envisioned as receiving systems innately tuned to their Creator's wavelength.

Human beings who live and move and have their being in God as the ground of all things have evolved as organisms capable of receiving meaningful information from God. Only humans with their highly evolved ever active stream of consciousness can pick up and understand the ideas, images and emotions that convey moral and spiritual meanings. Yet in many conditions the signals received will be full of static and noise—incomplete, garbled, incorrect or meaningless. Those persons suffering severe brain impairments or mental diseases will not be capable of normal reception. They either cannot receive information or they cannot exert enough normal decoding or self-regulation to make sense of their thoughts and feelings. They may be permanently off the air.

It is also true that normal, unimpaired persons are free enough to cultivate ears that do not hear by choosing to stifle, silence or suppress any promptings or signals that give evidence of God's reality. The religiously "tone-deaf" may be "frozen," "hardened" or "congenitally anaesthetic" (to use some terms from William James). Unbelievers may find themselves impervious to religious experience for various reasons, and may choose to remain incommunicado. A free creature can attend to transcendent signals of the More, or refuse to. It is easy to direct attention away from subtle stimuli. Even an immobile infant can control the flow of her incoming information by averting her gaze or turning her eyes away from her mother's face. While humans may be innately prepared receptors for religious signals, it is still necessary to choose to pay attention to perceptions of spiritual realities. Perhaps only sudden and acute pain or signals of imminent danger can always compel and capture attention. God's still, small voice has to be carefully attended to.

Surely, too, other persons with different temperaments and living in auspicious cultural conditions will always find it easier to be open to religious experiences. They may be more innately ready than others to be open to all experience, and to spiritual experiences in particular. Mystics have been compared to great artists in their abilities to receive spiritual signals and to create the words and images that convey spiritual meaning to others.[64] Mystics, like artists, also must discipline themselves to pay attention to what has not yet taken form. The patterns of information received of spiritual things is invisible, for all creativity consists of making invisible signals into patterns of meaning.

Even secular scientists affirm the existence of active information consisting of meaningful patterns that cannot be seen, touched, smelled or tasted.[65] Yet information is the ground and guide for ordering many developmental and communication processes. Information or meaningful signals or codes can be embodied in different media from DNA to the syntax and structure of language. The human organism receives and transmits information through many different systems with varying degrees of conscious awareness. Most of the information that floods into the human organism is being implicitly processed by the brain/mind below the level of explicit awareness. We can conceive of human consciousness as existing in a sea of information, or to use William James's language, reality consists of information fields existing within fields. Humans have evolved a conscious mind that seeks to discover, receive, make sense of and convey the information that comes to us through many channels of reception and through many capacities. Surely the God of truth uses many explicit and implicit channels to reach us in individual and social contexts, from the heights of reason to explicit encounters with people preaching the word, to the cloudy depths of individual consciousness. In the case of the individual, William James gives a special potency to implicit capacities of consciousness. James writes, "But just as our primary wide-awake consciousness throws open our senses to the touch of things material, so it is logically conceivable that if there be higher spiritual agencies that can directly touch us, the psychological condition of their doing so might be our possession of a subconscious region which alone should yield access to them. The hubbub of the waking life might close a door which in the dreamy Subliminal might remain ajar or open."[66] When individuals are converted they often look back and see the ways that, all along, God has provided them with inviting clues from within and without.

From a theological perspective, it can be argued that religious signals should emerge into ordinary everyday consciousness in subtle indirect ways. If God seeks to be a lover and a friend in a free and mutual relationship of love, then communication and invitations from active information must remain subtle.[67] Otherwise, creatures and creation would be coercively overwhelmed by the transcendent light of God's divine energy. Moses spoke to God but could not meet God face to face and live. So God tenderly protected Moses in a hidden cleft of a rock as God passed by so that only God's back could be glimpsed. Even so, after encounters with God, Moses' face was so frighteningly radiant that he had to wear a veil. Some enveloping cloud, darkness, indirectness or subtle ambiguity may be required in divine-human encounters if human beings are not to be burned up and consumed. Divine tact and courtesy ensures that God will have friends. and not stunned prostrated slaves.

Intuitions are one subtle implicit means of receiving information, because they spontaneously emerge into the stream of consciousness from we know not where. Intuitions are celebrated as the genesis of scientific discoveries as well as artistic creations. Ancient Greeks thought of the Muses as the source of flashes of insight. Such sudden inspirations are then available for sustained efforts of critical analysis and development. The critique and development takes work. So too, really good ideas, hunches, hypotheses and feelings only emerge into a mind prepared to receive them by previous processes of information gathering and attentive reflection. Conscious feelings of emotions are one important type of intuitive signals. Indeed, individual emotions have been called a way of being tacitly informed about the external and internal environment. The information that comes from emotions is crucial in conveying personal relevance and values to an individual. Whenever the emotional system in the brain becomes damaged or distorted, then so does our practical reasoning.[68] When all is functioning well, the intuitions, perceptions, thoughts, emotions and images that emerge into the stream of consciousness will be reflected upon or explored, checked or experimentally tested to prove or disprove the validity of an insight or event.[69]

Many psychologists have noted that humans spontaneously and quickly respond to stimuli in the environment in a primary response system and then can follow this initial response with a secondary process that employs the human ability to reflect and consider meanings in a more careful, more cognitive and more emotionally developed way.[70] The activation of the secondary system would include the processes of discernment, diagnosis or other forms of prudential and practical judgment. But the primary intuitive emergence of a new thought or idea or feeling may follow the same path in every experience—whether heralding triviality, unexceptional musing, creative novelty or madness. When Nobel laureate John Nash of *A Beautiful Mind* was asked why he, a scientist, believed his schizophrenic delusions of aliens and so on, he replied, "Because the ideas I had about supernatural beings came to me the same way that my mathematical ideas did. So I took them seriously."[71] The grandiose delusions and hallucinations of pathological processes may come into the mind just as other intuitions, thoughts or feelings. This is why every seeker of reliable knowledge faces the challenge of reflective testing in order to discriminate the valid signals from irrelevant chance signals, errors or other noise. Humility and listening to others in the search for truth should follow the emergence of the spontaneous thought or feeling, whether in science, art or religion. No seeker comes to the discovery of knowledge without the willingness to learn more than they now know, and to consider the possibility that at this point they may be mistaken or deceived in the information received.

New studies of hallucinations have reported the difficulty of discriminating a pathological reception of information from the unusual act of creative imagination.[72] Only by exercising judgment about the context and the whole quality of a person's mental and social functioning can a diagnosis of mental illness be made. No brain scan can (as yet) point to a definitive mark of a false perception. Over a century ago the philosopher Charles Peirce pointed out that the only way to tell hallucinations from valid perceptions "is that rational predictions based on the hallucination will likely be falsified. But this is a difference in the way they relate to other perceptions and not a difference in the nature of the perceptions themselves."[73] Obviously, when many observers can reach a consensus on the nature of a perception, it is more likely to lead to accurate predictions. But what if many observers do not concur in the perception? Time may be needed to sift and see what is developing. Some spiritually sensitive psychiatrists have been willing to grant that strange nonconsensual perceptions that intrude into the consciousness of people in a life crisis may signal "a spiritual emergency" rather than a psychotic mental illness.[74] The present chaos may signal the growth of a new level of psychological integration.

Think here of St. Ignatius's disturbed and psychologically turbulent path to conversion. Moreover, it is now being noticed that many great and creative leaders in religion and art have experienced voices or visions that today might be quickly classed as pathological.[75] Socrates, for instance, reported that he had a "daemon," or a voice, that told him what not to do.

Psychiatrists open to spiritual realities have begun to explore different levels of human consciousness and religious experience. They use different instruments such as brain-imaging techniques, questionnaires and self-report. Such psychological explorations have often been inspired by the spread in the West of Buddhism and other Eastern religions. Such researchers are willing to investigate the claim that there exist other fields of consciousness beyond the limited awareness of everyday conscious functioning and that these other levels of consciousness can be accessed by the brain, especially by the brains of skilled meditators. Brain-imaging techniques have been used to give evidence that the brain innately possesses abilities to achieve states of higher consciousness with a perceived communion with "absolute universal being." Two founders of what they call neurotheology sum up their studies and report on other work that has been done in their book *Why God Won't Go Away*.[76] Newberg and D'Aquili conclude that the mystical states they

93

have studied are "not the result of emotional mistakes or simple wishful thinking, but were associated instead with a series of observable neurological events that, while unusual, are not outside the range of normal brain function. In other words, mystical experience is biologically, observably and scientifically real."[77]

The innate human capacity for such states is considered to explain the origin of religions by many investigating the psychology of religion.[78] William James also believed these charismatic experiences of religious geniuses were the foundation of religions. Newberg and D'Aquili explain the perseverance of pervasiveness of religion to the power of rituals to innately trigger transcendent experiences. When intense arousal systems and quiescent systems are highly stimulated together or in sequence, mystical experiences of unity and ecstasy can ensue. These immediately luminous or numinous states described by William James and Rudolf Otto can now be observed neurologically and biochemically. The humanly perceived experience of receiving information from higher fields of consciousness and making contact with absolute unitary being is not so far-fetched if it is seen to be a neurologically real occurrence. Most challenging for modern skeptics is the claim that intense religious experience can be seen as different from pathological mental illness.

94

Newberg and D'Aquili claim that genuine religious experience differs in quality and effects from the diseased symptoms of hallucinations and voices.[79] Diseased or impaired functioning consists of experience that is involuntary, fragmented, incoherent, grandiose, irritable or distressing. Authentic mystical states, by contrast, bring joy, peace, humility and a greater energy for life. Christian mystics would testify to these findings. Ordinary believers like myself can also attest that from a qualitative point of view there is little problem in telling the difference between a horrific panic attack and an awe-inspiring sense of Christ's loving presence. Genuine religious experience produces trust in God's goodness and physical and mental health. Recently, other investigators of religious experience have gathered a body of empirical research that demonstrates the positive benefits of regular religious experience.[80] Hallucinations do not produce better mental functioning, and other mental illnesses make persons more open to physical disease. The observation that religion is innate to human beings and produces better social functioning has been extended backward in time to human evolutionary processes. The claim has been put forward that because religion can produce positive adaptive group functioning, it has persisted and been selected throughout human history.[81] Religion motivates and organizes cooperative and constructive activities. Destructive religious experiences may have existed but give way to better-adapted faiths. An argument from utility does not prove reality, but it is still surprising to see hard-core evolutionary biologists and brain scientists coming up with positive views of religious experiences. Perhaps these developments signal a turn away from hostile reductionist materialistic theories that have long dominated academic elites.

Scientists may someday admit two sources of influence on human consciousness. In addition to acknowledging the ways that everyday consciousness can be influenced or controlled by information coming from *below* in the biochemical, physiological systems of the organism, psychologists may also grant the power and influence of top-down information that comes from *beyond* the individual. No one doubts that pathology and mentally diseased brains and bodies produce intrusions of false information into consciousness arising from malfunctioning or disassociated brain regions, but that is only part of the story. Admittedly, anxiety attacks, obsessive compulsions, psychoses and other disabling disorders can appear and produce hallucinations and other symptoms in consciousness, but this will not be seen as the only explanation for religious experience. Artistic creativity, positive emotions, altruism and transcendent spiritual promptings may also be granted more significance in mystic inspiration. The intuitive emergence into everyday consciousness of novel information may be destructively pathological, neutrally trivial or intensely creative, benign and spiritually inspiring. In the best-case scenarios, the "subliminal" mind that implicitly can become explicit in everyday awareness may be tuned to higher mathematical truths or creative art and musical patterns—or to more intense insights into God's nature and love for creation.[82]

But why voices, or visions? While there are many channels of information reception and many different kinds of human intelligence, the capacities for language, imagination and emotions are central to gathering and processing information. It is hardly surprising that new information emerges into awareness as emotionally charged voices, dialogues or visions. Indeed, everyone who has mastered language hears inner voices and is engaged in silent invisible inner dialogues with others. Persons mentally replay conversations or imagine new ones. Bernard Shaw, in his drama about Joan of Arc, has her say of her voices, "But doesn't everyone have voices?" Yes, they do, although Shaw's effort to resolve the problem of Joan's uniqueness was too evasive, since she explicitly claimed that her voices came from God. Recently it has been revealed in letters of Mother Teresa of Calcutta that she had experiences of "inner locutions" with Jesus while trying to decide whether to initiate her charitable ministry. Obviously certain religious geniuses devoting their attention and their lives to

God will receive more vivid messages and more insistent voices and visions than other people. Their sustained efforts to make contact with the More of reality will bear fruit. Yet all humans with functioning brains can be seen as innate religious information receptors. As migrating birds can receive information from the earth's magnetic fields, so too, humans can become aware of spiritual communication. Birds fly in a flock and human beings are also innately social, providing us with another useful analogy for understanding religious experience.

The Conversation

The basic social and emotional character of the human species leads to a realization that religious experience arises from participating in a divine-human conversation. Human beings are innately programmed for interpersonal relationships from the beginning of life.[83] Infants seek and recognize human faces and the smell of their mothers. Emotional attachment produces modes of communication long before speech develops. Human interpersonal preverbal conversations can take place through touch, smell, gesture, sounds, sight, hearing, mutual activity and mutual emotions. Emotions are not only contagious but they are part of a dance of emotional attunement or appropriately matched responses between the infant and a sensitive caretaker. Adults continue these dances of attunement. Emotions give us tacit information about the internal and external environment and are central to human communication.[84] With the capacity for speech, interpersonal communication can become more expansive, abstract, symbolic and emotionally nuanced. Both the content and the context broaden and deepen but remain fused with emotion and body language. It is appropriate to think of religious experience as interpersonal communication or an I-Thou relationship. Certainly this is not a new idea. Many thinkers today, from the Jewish philosopher Martin Buber onward, see the dialogue with God, creation and creatures as the necessary path of religious growth.[85] Christians who affirm God as Trinity will be drawn to the model of religious experience as an eternal interpersonal communion. For Christians, human beings are created in the divine image and so are prepared for an eternal giving and receiving of differentiated persons in unity. God will be affirmed to be reaching out to beloved creatures to bring them into the eternal conversation and communion of God's family life. It is easy to envision God as the loving parent seeking to make contact and continue the intimate dialogue that begins in infancy and lasts to the end of life and beyond.

In a human interpersonal encounter it is important that each person be free to act and to respond without restraint. Parents must not be overintrusive or too dominating with their children. If parents are too coercive, they deny their children the chance to take initiative and exercise the agency and sensitive responses they need to develop. In conversing, two individuals who are actively participating can engender new understanding of one another as well as new knowledge. Conversations also bring intimacy and joy. In fact, two people can be so carried away or transported in an intense conversation that everyday consciousness is left behind. These moments of being transported out of self are instances of the "flow" already mentioned. The flow of mutual emotional experience in conversation offers an ordinary example of the self-forgetting rapture that many saints and mystics describe. Time stands still in the delightful encounter, and physical surroundings recede from awareness. These experiences of joy and communion have been seen as a foretaste of the heavenly communion of God's family. Augustine famously describes the way his conversation with Monica at Ostia, when they talked of heavenly things, seemed to carry them up to a joyful union with the Spirit.

But again, the analogy of a conversation can help explain how errors and misunderstandings can occur within religious experience. Within conversations, which generally provide real effective communication with others, a misreading of signals can still occur. This may happen more easily when one of the persons in the dialogue has less knowledge, experience, emotional maturity, sense of humor or powers of attentive comprehension than the other. Parents who have listened to their young children attempt to recount the plot of a movie they have seen recognize the effects on communication of discrepancies in maturity. Adults can also remember some of their own childhood misinterpretations and misreadings of conversations. It takes emotional intelligence to become adept at intimate communication. Even though adults innately speak baby talk to infants and try to simplify their messages, many mistakes in transmission occur. It seems quite reasonable to see that God's efforts to communicate and be present to beloved creatures can be marred by the difficulties of communication between persons. God as the most loving, ardently desiring and nurturing Communicator is willing to go to any lengths to pursue mutual understanding, but even God can be stymied by human emotional limitations. As Abbot Thomas Keating has written, "Unfortunately, when we are not available to the Spirit, we think that the Spirit is absent."[86] Obviously, too, a human being's freely chosen obtuseness or rebelliousness can skew conversation and understanding. The gospels depict Christ's frustrations with the incomprehension of his disciples, which echo Yahweh's complaints about his people in the Old Testament. The divine empathy never fails in steadfast attentiveness, but human beings do.

It is also obvious that if one person in a conversation is suffering from some serious clinical impairment of the organism, such as deafness, brain disease, drug poisoning or some disordered cognitive and emotional function, then the conversation will be even more distorted. Misunderstandings and misperceptions will be inevitable. The experiences that psychotic persons can have of God speaking to them in terrifying voices with horrible visions may be examples of a completely misconstrued communication taking place. Normal persons can gain empathy for these pathological situations by remembering the grogginess and confusion they experienced when waking up from anesthesia. Trying to talk and answer one's physician or one's family can be futile if not anxiety-producing. Even the process of awakening from a deep sleep or nightmare involves impaired ability to communicate. In normal unimpaired persons there can exist other befogging conditions, arising from sin, rebelliousness or carelessness, in which no communication with God (or anyone else) can make much headway. By contrast, extreme moments of desperation, fear and pain may sometimes clarify the mind wonderfully and turn attention to the need for help. In emergencies habitual defenses and arrogant self-sufficiency can fall away. The extremity of the need produces a cry for help that serves to disclose the divine Presence. Many psalms contain these cries to God, with the answering experience of God's saving response.

102

Powerful experiences of interpersonal relationship can produce human transformations as well as prototypical religious experiences. A group of psychoanalytic thinkers friendly to religion have explored these processes and moved beyond Freudian perspectives upon religion as defensive regression.[87] New psychoanalytic explorations of the birth of the self claim that a human self emerges from a child's earliest experiences of nurturing by others. The "I" of human consciousness is seen to arise from the dialogue with the "Thou" of the mothering one. The self is created from an inner genetic predisposition and program that flowers within a primordial conversation and experience of care and communion. This early coming to be of one's self is an exhilarating experience of creative confirmation and transformation. The powerful joyful experience of being psychologically born is a mysterious event—something new emerges, and becomes a model of the "sacred" dimension in human experience. Throughout life human selves will seek to reinvoke these emotionally powerful sacred transformations in other creative relationships. Religious experiences of mystery and sacredness are the most powerful examples of transformation.

As James Jones, one of the psychoanalysts positively exploring religion, puts it, "Such transforming moments are not recreations of memories of past events but rather represent a return to the foundational experiences of human life. Such a return to the well-spring of our conscious existence carries the hope and the possibility of metamorphosis, of reworking or transforming aspects of ourselves and our relation to the world."[88] Such an analysis of sacred experience arising from the birth of the self in relationship is consonant with Christian worship of God as Trinity. Christians affirm that ultimate reality consists of a divine "I Am" who lives in an eternal interpersonal communion and dialogue of three persons in one. It seems no surprise, then, that a human creature should psychologically be born from experiences of interpersonal dialogue. An "I" is born from an "I-Thou dialogue" and becomes part of the "we" of the human family. Religious experiences reenact and resonate with the sacred transformation of the creation, or the process that brings something from nothing. As in the beginning of human lives, individual selves are differentiated and born at the same time that interpersonal communion and union with others are enlarged. The desires of the human heart to be affirmed as an "I" and to be in union with others are met. If religious experience gains its force from simultaneously strengthening a sense of agency and a sense of communion, then it will have power founded on the beginning of every human life. Religion will last as long as human beings are born, nurtured and desire to know. The most positive experiences of humankind generate religious experience, which can no longer be dismissed as only defensive or delusional.

Now I can see that religious experience, even the most intense religious experiences of hearing voices and seeing visions, can be the happy result of innate human cognitive predispositions of our embodied and socially embedded human nature. Evolutionary developments of the brain and body produce readiness for both concrete and transcendent experiences of others and of the More beyond. Reductive materialistic views of religion as pathology or wish fulfillment have not won the day. Today it is possible for secular psychology to provide evidence that human beings are innately ready and responsive to God and God's call. What skeptics read as irrational pathological projection upon reality can be convincingly seen as the reality of God-readiness in the human race. How I wish that I had known more about the sources of religious experience during my earlier bouts of self-doubt! Knowing more about the depths of the human mind and heart could have helped me accept the reality of my own powerful experiences of God's loving presence A fuller understanding of differential diagnosis and the discernment of spirits could have reassured me.

Of course it is also of vital interest to note that the original primary dialogue that begets the self and the sense of the sacred is with a woman. Does this reassessment of the birth of the sacred have any bearings on our understanding of women's religious experience?

The Challenge of Women's Religious Experience

A defense of the validity of religious experience basically applies to both men and women despite the fact that religious women have been more subject to reductionist dismissals. Still, the question can arise of whether women have unique features and characteristics in their religious experience. Such a question about gender can stir up a hornet's nest in and out of religious thought. Many feminist thinkers emphasize how much alike men and women are (equality feminists), while others wish to focus on differences or essential differences between the genders (difference feminists or romantic feminists). Those who advocate the notion of essential gender differences will want to find unique feminine characteristics in women's religious experiences, since women's special gifts must be uniquely their own and celebrated as such. Womanly insights into God and religious truth should speak to us in special and penetrating ways through time. Women who are equal in the sight of God will still give glory to God through their essential nature and in the complementary relationship to males.[89]

I am of the feminist persuasion that emphasizes how alike men and women are in their mental, moral and spiritual capacities. I judge the evidence of both psychology and Christian theology to show that differences among individuals are not so much the result of gender but are more usually caused by the multitude of other individual differences that always exist among persons. Individual differences have more importance than gender differences. Individuals are more themselves in their particular constitutions, personalities and moral choices than they are like other women or other men of the same gender.[90] Gender differences will be minor compared to other characteristics. Individuals qua individuals will be shaped by their innate intellectual, emotional and temperamental characteristics, interacting with their individual actions within the historical cultural conditions within which they live and operate.[91] Genes are crucial but there are a lot of them that are not associated with gender. And experience, like genes, can change the brain and body.

Gender will not be the dominating characteristic of one's moral, intellectual or spiritual life. Theologically it has been asserted that "in Christ there is neither male nor female, Jew or Greek, slave or free." All humanity is saved in Christ. All humans made in the image of God will be members of the human species and called to build up the human community in complementary ways that do not relate to gender. As an embodied individual progresses from embryo to newborn to child to adolescent to adult to frail elder, the body will change and so will the potential of biological gender functions. The mating and reproductive period of life is only one stage of life. The way a human individual's embodied stages are lived will depend upon individual differences interacting with class, ethnicity and other cultural conditions. Within this reading, women's religious experiences would not necessarily share any essential characteristics.

Yet the so-called "difference feminists" have a point when they claim that through millions of years of evolution biological and environmental conditions must have operated to shape women's natures in certain ways. From birth a gender socialization begins that takes into account women's adult biological capacities to mate, become pregnant and bear children. Adult women's power to give or withhold erotic pleasure to men and to nurture offspring will be a biological reality undergirding any construction of a cultural identity for women. The small number of women who will be single or become vowed to virginity and religious life can hardly change the salience of the basic fact of female erotic, reproductive and nurturing power. Women will tend to internalize these distinct female gender images, even if there exist no actual genetically determined sexual or maternal behaviors. We also know for sure that emotional attachment is innate to our social species and that every child alive has been born of a woman and received female care and nourishment. If these experiences become the foundation of the experience of both the emergence of self and the sense of the sacred, they will have symbolic force.

Certainly when you look at all primate and human societies, it becomes clear that the mother-infant bond is primary. Without attentive mothering and care of the young, no primate group survives. The long period of dependence in the human species ensures that emotional bonding and a great deal of learning and socialization take place within the kin group. Mothers may have the help of other females and some help from fathers, but the identification of women with nurture, comfort, care and protection is ingrained in all human societies. Women may also have to punish, discipline and set boundaries upon the young in order to raise an acceptable child who can function in the larger group, but first the infant and child must survive and flourish. One noted analysis of the core of the function of modern mothers has said that mothers must protect and encourage individual flourishing as well as produce an acceptably socialized child—all at the same time.[92] Since these functions may be in direct conflict, mothers or their nurturing helpers have to be patient, persevering, cheerful and skilled in persuading offspring to behave without using harmful coercive measures.

Mothering is a complex activity requiring many different skills and capacities. The more skilled and attentive the mother, the better the outcome for the offspring. In nonhuman primate troops the dominance of the mother will determine the status and life prospects of the offspring.

Some evolutionary psychologists would claim that since women have had the primary care of children they will be genetically predisposed to react to threat in a unique way. If you know about "fight or flight" responses to threat, you are ready to hear of "tend and befriend" strategies. Some preliminary research has reported that females react to danger by quieting and soothing their offspring and affiliating with a group for protection. If females fight or flee, they endanger the survival of their progeny and themselves. Better to calm down and blend into friendly networks.

The more classic male "fight or flight" response to threat activates the sympathetic nervous system with cascading adrenaline hormones secreted into the bloodstream. These highly aroused animals are mobilized to attack or flee. But in our civilized world, men cannot easily fight or flee from threats. The resulting buildup of frustrated stress responses has been blamed for the high rates of male cardiovascular disease and the fact that men live, on the average, seven and a half years less than women. Men also seem less adept at handling personal relationships and reading the emotional signals necessary for interactions.

Females can have sympathetic arousal to stress as well, but the new model of tending and befriending proposes that women more often respond with surges of sedating, anxiety-calming oxytocin, which is enhanced by their estrogen. Such hormones induce females to remain calm, nurture their offspring, and seek support from others. Since assaults and threats to females often come from aggressive males, even from a sexual partner, females facing stress turn to female networks of kin and friends. This results in female tendencies to create and maintain cooperative female groups in order to enhance their own safety and their offspring's survival. Thus women as compared to males, are more likely to tend and befriend, to create and maintain social networks and to be less threatened by crowding. Maternal investments and befriending strategies are part of an innate attachment-nurturing system that operates in both infants and their caretakers. Such behavior rests on the neuro-endocrine underpinnings of oxytocin, estrogen and opioid mechanisms.

Other psychological gender differences that have been observed are earlier female language acquisition, more skill in decoding emotions, more reported religious experiences and more clinical depression. Of course, other medical prognoses can be due to gender differences in hormones and physiological makeup, but in human development the biological, psychological and social are fused. Many medical conditions such as clinical depression may be caused by social factors, and it is surely the case that, until recently, more women have been subject to male-dominated cultural conditions and have had less control of their lives. Domestic abuse of weaker females by males has been observed in primate groups and is endemic in many human cultures. Women are vulnerable to rape and have suffered more social constraints in most cultures.

Given the evolutionary and cultural history of women in the Christian West, I think we could hazard some tentative generalities about women's religious experiences. While equality feminists can be correct in stressing the primary importance of individual characteristics, other gender universals may play a part. If it is true that the mother-child relationship is the primary interpersonal bond affecting human development and marks the genesis of both the self and a sense of the sacred, then women have been greatly favored by evolution in their reproductive and nurturing potentialities for positive creativity. No wonder there have been so many mother goddesses in human history. Women's enabling power arises from their ability to create new life and sustain family kin groups. By internalizing maternal images young women may be more disposed to developing psychological nurturing and to creating caring relationships.

Women's traditional roles may have made them ready to receive the gospel good news of God's loving care for humankind. Christianity gained many converts among women because of the appeal of its basic messages about the value of human life and the importance of women's roles in the family.[93] Women's embeddedness in embodiment and interpersonal emotional experience would make them appreciate the incarnation and its validation of the body. Moreover, if personal relationships are the ultimate reality of God as Trinity, women's concrete experiences of constantly being in relationship would prepare them for community life in the church. Love of every kind, familial and erotic, must always have played a large part in female lives and socialization, so it is not surprising to find women using these images to express their love of God and God's love for creatures. While males could resonate to ideas of Jesus as mother, women would find them particularly convincing.[94] Women must also have appreciated the practice of speaking of the Holy Spirit as feminine.

The knowledge that the Holy Spirit freely inspires women outside of the church's hierarchical channels ensures that women could have an important role in prophecy and the life of the church. Women's association with the Spirit's freedom combined with women's long association with children can also account for female mystics' use of childlike and playful imagery, a practice that so offended proponents of religious gravitas and seriousness. Fortunately a lack of official social roles in the church and the world can have its compensations; women have been freer to be emotional, playful and take risks in their religious experience. Women can dare to be thought mad or neurotic or excessively emotional, like lovers and children. Has not Jesus pointed to great lovers and to the child as the way to the kingdom? The gospels have always validated the worth and great happiness granted to those who are poor in spirit, those who hunger and thirst, or mourn. Those who seek with the most fervor will be most open to being filled and will be the most grateful. Women for all of the above reasons may be open to the Spirit and consequently be gifted with joys and blessings.

So too, women's religious experience has often been prophetic in anticipating and moving the church forward to a fuller understanding of God's maternal mercies toward all. Women's openness to emotional religious experience, especially in intense forms of mystical manifestations, has borne fruit in wisdom. Ron Hansen, a novelist writing on the history of the stigmata, has noted that "women are seven times more likely than men to get the stigmata"; he speculates that this disproportion may "be God's way of illustrating the importance of women in Christ's ministry and of correcting the imbalance in Holy Scripture, where a far higher proportion of men have their voices heard."[95] From a theological perspective one can affirm that women's religious experience has been a strategic work of the Spirit in the world.

Women who hear voices and see visions and have prophetic and intimate religious experiences have given witness to God's justice and equality while affirming God's maternal love. As in the past, so into the future. Christian women gain authority in the church and the world through their Spirit-filled religious experiences. This is right, good and fitting for a religion that begins with one woman's belief in God's good word to her. Mary tests her angelic experience by asking how this can be, but, being satisfied in her discernment, she places her complete trust in God. Mary's faith in her experience of God's bestowal of love ensures the salvation of the world.

NOTES

1. Jean Baker Miller, *Toward a New Psychology for Women* (Boston: Beacon Press, 1973).

2. Jane Schaberg, "The Resurrection of Mary Magdalene: Legends, Apocrypha, and the Christian Testament," CrossCurrents (spring 2002): 82.

3. Elisabeth Schüssler Fiorenza, *In Memory of Her: A Feminist Theological Reconstruction of Christian Origins* (New York: Crossroad, 1989); and Mary R. Thompson, S.S.M.N., *Mary of Magdala: Apostle and Leader* (New York: Paulist Press, 1995).

4. Françoise Meltzer, *For Fear of the Fire: Joan of Arc and the Limits of Subjectivity* (Chicago: University of Chicago Press, 2001), p. 14.

5. Amy Hollywood, *Sensible Ecstasy: Mysticism, Sexual Difference, and the Demands of History* (Chicago: University of Chicago Press, 2002), p. 5.

6. Cathleen Medwick, *Teresa of Avila: The Progress of a Soul* (New York: Alfred A. Knopf, 1999), p. 260.

7. William James, *The Varieties of Religious Experience* (New York: Penguin Books, [1902] 1985), pp. 347–48.

8. Quoted by Matthew Fox in his foreword, p. 22, to *Hildegard of Bingen's Scivias* (Santa Fe, N.M.: Bear & Company, 1986).

9. Oliver Sacks, "The Visions of Hildegard," in *The Man Who Mistook His Wife for a Hat: And Other Clinical Tales* (New York: Harper & Row, Perennial Library Edition,1987), p.168.

10. J. Allan Hobson, M.D., *The Chemistry of Conscious States: How the Brain Changes Its Mind* (Boston: Little, Brown & Company, 1994); Harry T. Hunt, *The Multiplicity of Dreams: Memory, Imagination, and Consciousness* (New Haven: Yale University Press, 1989).

11. Hobson, *The Chemistry of Conscious States,* p. 4.

12. Daniel M. Wegner, *The Illusion of Conscious Will* (Cambridge, Mass.: MIT Press, 2002).

13. James W. Jones, *Contemporary Psychoanalysis & Religion* (New Haven: Yale University Press, 1991).

14. Helena Deutsch, *The Psychology of Women: A Psychoanalytic Interpretation* (New York: Grune & Stratton, 1944).

15. James, *The Varieties of Religious Experience,* p.8.

117

16. Howard Gardner, *Multiple Intelligences: The Theory in Practice* (New York: Basic Books, 1993).

17. Daniel Goleman, *Emotional Intelligence* (New York: Bantam Books, 1995).

18. Stephen Pinker, *How the Mind Works* (New York: W. W. Norton, 1997), p. 557.

19. Ibid., p. 560.

20. Wegner, *The Illusion of Conscious Will,* p. 226.

21. Joseph de Rivera and Theodore R. Sarbin, eds., *Believed-In Imaginings: The Narrative Construction of Reality* (Washington, D.C.: American Psychological Association, 1998).

22. Daniel L. Schacter, *Searching for Memory: The Brain, the Mind, and the Past* (New York: Basic Books, 1996).

23. Wayne Proudfoot, *Religious Experience* (Berkeley: University of California Press, 1985).

24. Ibid., p. 236.

25. Quoted in James Thrower, *Religion: The Classical Theories* (Washington, D.C.: Georgetown University Press, 1999), p. 140.

26. Kai Nielsen, "Is Religion the Opium of the People? Marxianism and Religion," in D. Z. Phillips, ed., *Can Religion Be Explained Away?* (New York: St. Martin's Press, 1996), 177–223.

27. Ann Taves, *Fits, Trances and Visions: Experiencing Religion and Explaining Experience*

from Wesley to James (Princeton, N.J.: Princeton University Press, 1999).

28. See the writings of R. D. Laing, A. Esterson and David Cooper.

29. Phyllis Chesler, *Women and Madness* (New York: Four Walls Eight Windows, 1997).

30. Evan B. Howard, *Affirming the Touch of God: A Psychological and Philosophical Exploration of Christian Discernment* (New York: University Press of America, 2000).

31. Avery Dulles, "Faith and Revelation," in Francis Schüssler Fiorenza and John P. Galving, eds., *Systematic Theology: Roman Catholic Perspectives,* vol. I (Minneapolis, Minn.: Fortress Press, 1991), p.109.

32. Nicholas Lash, *Believing in One God Three Ways* (Notre Dame, Ind.: University of Notre Dame Press, 1993), p.10.

33. Donald L. Gelpi, S.J., *The Turn to Experience in Contemporary Theology* (New York: Paulist Press, 1994), p. 2.

34. Owen Flanagan, *Consciousness Reconsidered* (Cambridge, Mass: MIT Press, 1992) and Joseph F. Rychlak, *In Defense of Human Consciousness* (Washington D.C.: American Psychological Association, 1997).

35. Rychalk, *In Defense of Human Consciousness;* Merlin Donald, *A Mind So Rare: The Evolution of Human Consciousness* (New York: W. W. Norton & Company, 2001).

36. William James, *The Principles of Psychology,* vol. I (New York: Dover Publications, 1950).

37. Michael Lewis and Linda Michalson, *Children's Emotions and Moods* (New York: Plenum Press, 1983), p. 88; also see Antonio Damasio, *The Feeling of What Happens: Body and Emotion in the Making of Consciousness* (New York: Harcourt Brace,1999).

38. Mihalyi Csikszentimihalyi, *Flow: The Psychology of Optimal Experience* (New York: Harper & Row, 1990).

39. Louis Roy, O.P., *Transcendent Experiences: Phenomenology and Critique* (Toronto: University of Toronto Press, 2001); Robert K. C. Forman, ed., *The Innate Capacity: Mysticism, Psychology, and Philosophy* (New York: Oxford University Press, 1998).

40. James, *Varieties;* and Evelyn Underhill, *Mysticism: A Study in the Nature and Development of Man's Spiritual Consciousness* (New York: Noonday Press, 1955).

41. Charles Taylor, *Varieties of Religion Today: William James Revisited* (Cambridge, Mass.: Harvard University Press, 2002), pp. 23–26.

42. Rudolf Otto, *The Idea of the Holy* (Oxford: Oxford University Press, [1923] 1958).

43. Rodney Stark, "A Taxonomy of Religious Experience," in Bernard Spilka and Daniel N.

McIntosh, eds., *The Psychology of Religion: Theoretical Approaches* (New York: Westview Press, 1997), p. 210.

44. Ibid., p. 210.

45. Spilka and McIntosh, *The Psychology of Religion*, p. 234.

46. Ibid.

47. John Thiel, *Senses of Tradition: Continuity and Development in Catholic Faith* (New York: Oxford University Press, 2000).

48. John F. Haught, *God After Darwin: A Theology of Evolution* (Boulder, Colo.: Westview Press, 2000).

49. William R. Stoeger, S.J., "God and Time: The Action and Life of the Triune God in the World," *Theology Today* 55/3 (October 1998): 368.

50. Warren S. Brown, Nancey Murphy, and H. Newton Malony, eds., *Whatever Happened to the Soul? Scientific and Theological Portraits of Human Nature* (Minneapolis, Minn.: Fortress Press,1998).

51. Elizabeth A. Johnson, C.S.J., "Does God Play Dice? Divine Providence and Chance," *Theological Studies* 57/1 (March 1996): 3–18.

52. Lucien Richard, O.M.I, *Christ: The Self-Emptying of God* (New York: Paulist Press, 1997).

53. Lash, *Believing in One God Three Ways,* p. 101.

54. Charles E. Bouchard, O.P., "Recovering the Gifts of the Holy Spirit in Moral Theology," *Theological Studies* 63/3 (September 2002):539–58.

55. David Tracy, *Blessed Rage for Order* (San Francisco: Harper & Row, 1988), p. 183.

56. Johnson, "Does God Play Dice?"; Ann Pederson, *God, Creation, and All That Jazz: A Process of Composition and Improvisation* (St. Louis, Mo.: Chalice Press, 2001).

57. Haught, *God After Darwin*; Edward Farley, *Divine Empathy: A Theology of God* (Minneapolis, Minn.: Augsburg Fortress, 1996).

58. Tracy, *Blessed Rage*, p. 183.

59. Howard, *Affirming the Touch of God*; Michael Downey, *Understanding Christian Spirituality* (New York: Paulist Press, 1997).

60. Karl Rahner, *Visions and Prophecies* (New York: Herder & Herder, 1963).

61. Ibid., p. 36.

62. Ibid., p. 28.

63. Ibid.; see note on p. 29.

64. Underhill, *Mysticism*. Chapter 4 develops this analogy.

65. Pinker, *How the Mind Works*, pp. 25–26.

66. James, *Varieties*, p. 242.

67. John Polkinghorne, "God in Relation to Nature: Kenotic Creation and Divine Action," in *Faith, Science & Understanding* (New Haven: Yale University Press, 2000).

68. Antonio Damasio, *Descartes' Error: Emotion, Reason, and the Human Brain* (New York: Putnam, 1994).

69. Sidney Callahan, *In Good Conscience: Reason and Emotion in Moral Decision Making* (HarperSanFrancisco, 1991).

70. Timothy D. Wilson, *Strangers to Ourselves: Discovering the Adaptive Unconscious* (Cambridge Mass.: Harvard University Press, 2002).

71. Sylvia Nasar, *A Beautiful Mind: The Life of Mathematical Genius and Nobel Laureate John Nash* (New York: Simon & Schuster, 1998), p. 11.

72. R. P. Bentall, "The Illusion of Reality: A Review and Integration of Psychological Research on Hallucinations," *Psychological Bulletin* 107/1 (January 1990): 82–95.

73. Charles Peirce, "The Collected Papers of Charles Sanders Peirce, VII, p. 644," quoted in John K. Sheriff, *Charles Peirce's Guess at the Riddle* (Indianapolis, Ind.: Indiana University Press, 1994), p. 53.

74. David Lukoff, Frances Lu, M.D., and Robert Turner, M.D., "From Spiritual Emergency to Spiritual Problem: The Transpersonal Roots of the New DSM-IV Category," *Journal of Humanistic Psychology* 38/2 (spring 1998): 21–50; there are also Web sites for those seeking information on spiritual emergencies and the Spiritual Emergence Institute, complete with lists of sympathetic psychotherapists.

75. Mitchell B. Liester, "Inner Voices: Distinguishing Transcendent and Pathological Characteristics," *Journal of Transpersonal Psychology* 28/1(1996): 1–30.

76. Andrew Newberg, M.D., Eugene D'Aquili, M.C., Ph.D., and Vince Rause, *Why God Won't Go Away: Brain Science and the Biology of Belief* (New York: Ballantine Books, 2001).

77. Ibid., p. 7.

78. Robert K. C. Forman, *Mysticism, Mind, Consciousness* (Albany: State University of New York Press, 1999).

79. Newberg et al., *Why God Won't Go Away,* pp.111–13.

80. David B. Larson, J. P. Swyers, and M. E. McCullough, *Scientific Research on Spirituality and Health : A Consensus Report* (Rockville, Md.: National Institute of Healthcare Research,1997); Howard. G. Koenig, *The Healing Power of Faith* (New York: Simon & Schuster, 1999).

81. David Sloan Wilson, *Darwin's Cathedral: Evolution, Religion and the Nature of Society* (Chicago: University of Chicago Press, 2002).

82. Bernard McGinn, appendix, "Theoretical Foundations: The Modern Study of Mysticism," in *The Foundations of Mysticism: Origins to the Fifth Century* (New York: Crossroad, 1995), pp. 265–343.

83. Daniel N. Stern, *The Interpersonal World of the Infant* (New York: Basic Books, 1985).

84. Sidney Callahan, "The Psychology of Emotion and the Ethics of Care," in *Medicine and the Ethics of Care,* Diana Fritz Cates and Paul Lauritzen, eds. (Washington, D.C.: Georgetown University Press, 2001), pp.141–61.

85. Maurice Friedman, *Religion and Psychology: A Dialogical Approach* (New York: Paragon House, 1992).

86. Thomas Keating, *Fruits and Gifts of the Spirit* (New York: Lantern Books, 2000), p.15.

87. Jones, *Contemporary Psychoanalysis & Religion;* Ana-Maria Rizzuto, M.D., *The Birth of the Living God: A Psychoanalytic Study* (Chicago: University of Chicago Press, 1979); Robert Coles, *The Spiritual Life of Children* (Boston: Houghton Mifflin, 1990).

88. Jones, *Contemporary Psychoanalysis & Religion,* p. 123.

89. Pope John Paul II, *Mulieris Dignitatem (On the Dignity of Women).*

90. Sidney Callahan, "Self and Other in Feminist Thought," in *Duties to Others,* Courtney S. Campbell and B. Andrew Lustig, eds. (Boston: Kluwer Academic Publishers, 1994), pp. 55–69.

91. Alice H. Eagly and Wendy Wood, "The Origins of Sex Differences in Human Behavior Evolved Dispositions Versus Social Roles," *American Psychologist* 54/6 (June 1999): 408–23.

92. Sara Ruddick, "Maternal Thinking," in Joyce Trebilcot, ed., *Mothering* (Totowa N.J.: Rowman and Allanheld, 1984), pp. 213–30.

93. Rodney Stark, *The Rise of Christianity: A Sociologist Reconsiders History* (Princeton, N.J.: Princeton University Press, 1996).

94. Caroline Walker Bynum, *Jesus as Mother: Studies in the Spirituality of the High Middle Ages* (Berkeley: University of California Press, 1982).

95. Ron Hansen, *A Stay Against Confusion: Essays on Faith and Fiction* (New York: HarperCollins, 2001), p.180.

The Madeleva Lecture in Spirituality

This series, sponsored by the Center for Spirituality, Saint Mary's College, Notre Dame, Indiana, honors annually the woman who as president of the college inaugurated its pioneering graduate program in theology, Sister M. Madeleva, C.S.C.

1985
Monika K. Hellwig
Christian Women in a Troubled World

1986
Sandra M. Schneiders
Women and the Word

1987
Mary Collins
Women at Prayer

1988
Maria Harris
Women and Teaching

1989
Elizabeth Dreyer
Passionate Women: Two Medieval Mystics

1990
Joan Chittister, O.S.B.
Job's Daughters

1991
Dolores R. Leckey
Women and Creativity

1992
Lisa Sowle Cahill
Women and Sexuality

1993
Elizabeth A. Johnson
Women, Earth, and Creator Spirit

1994
Gail Porter Mandell
Madeleva: One Woman's Life

1995
Diana L. Hayes
Hagar's Daughters

1996
Jeanette Rodriguez
Stories We Live
Cuentos Que Vivimos

1997
Mary C. Boys
Jewish-Christian Dialogue

1998
Kathleen Norris
The Quotidian Mysteries

1999
Denise Lardner Carmody
An Ideal Church: A Meditation

2000
Sandra M. Schneiders
With Oil in Their Lamps

2001
Mary Catherine Hilkert
Speaking with Authority

2002
Margaret A. Farley
Compassionate Respect